Oh! Jesus, Help Me Over the Hump of My Rainbow

*To Pastor Hooks
All the Best
Ronie Rogers*

Oh! Jesus, Help Me Over the Hump of My Rainbow

Ronii Rogers

Copyright © 2008 by Ronii Rogers.

Library of Congress Control Number: 2008904685
ISBN: Hardcover   978-1-4363-4514-9
               Softcover   978-1-4363-4513-2

All rights reserved. No part of this book may be reproduced or transmitted in any form or by any means, electronic or mechanical, including photocopying, recording, or by any information storage and retrieval system, without permission in writing from the copyright owner.

This book was printed in the United States of America.

To order additional copies of this book, contact:
Xlibris Corporation
1-888-795-4274
www.Xlibris.com
Orders@Xlibris.com
48170

CONTENTS

Acknowledgment 7
Introduction 9

SECTION I
The Green Road

*"The **purpose** of life is a life of purpose."*
—Robert Byrne (1928-)—

Chapter 1	My Beginning	13
Chapter 2	Sisters	17
Chapter 3	Tiny Terror	20
Chapter 4	The Great Introduction	24
Chapter 5	My Best Friend	29
Chapter 6	First Steps of Liberty	36
	I have learned that	40

SECTION II
The Blue Road

*"**Experience** is a hard teacher. She gives the test first and the lessons afterwards."*
—Anonymous—

Chapter 7	My First Storm	43
Chapter 8	False Love	48
Chapter 9	My Greatest Loss	53
Chapter 10	Back in the Race	59
Chapter 11	All That Glitters Ain't Gold	67
Chapter 12	A Cheating Heart	73
	I have learned that	77

SECTION III
The Red Road

*"**Passion** impels our deeds; ideology supplies the explanations."*
—Mason Cooley (1927-2002)—

Chapter 13	Deceive Me If You Can	81
Chapter 14	Nothing Beats a Try . . . But	88
Chapter 15	On My Own	94
Chapter 16	My Friend—Adversity	100
Chapter 17	Like Father, Like Daughter	106
Chapter 18	And Baby Makes Three	111
Chapter 19	She Works Hard for the Money	118
	I have learned that . . .	124

SECTION IV
The Yellow Road

*"**Grace** is not a strange, magic substance which is subtly filtered into our souls to act as a kind of spiritual penicillin. Grace is unity, oneness within ourselves, oneness with God."*
—Thomas Merton (1915-1968)—

Chapter 20	Don't Get Mad, Get Even	127
Chapter 21	Charlie, My Charlie	131
Chapter 22	Gone, but Not Forgotten	136
Chapter 23	Veni, Vidi, Vici	143
Chapter 24	The Richness of Humility	150
Chapter 25	Grace Changes Everything	159
Chapter 26	Be Careful What You Ask For	168
	I have learned that . . .	179

Epilogue 181
Index 183

Acknowledgment

To my special friend Cleon, it was your initial suggestion eighteen years ago that *I should write a book,* which led me into this experience. Had it not been for your tenacious reminders over the years, this book would not have materialized. You insisted that I could *do it* and your encouraging words struck the proverbial match that lit my way out of a fog. I am eternally grateful for your friendship.

To my devoted sister Dee: I appreciate your *golden ears* that always made time to listen to me, the patience you had with me through every situation I shared with you, and the comfort you gave me when I needed a shoulder to lean on.

To my lifelong girlfriend Terri: Thank you for your never-ending words of encouragement and monthly pep talks. To my cousin Shirley: Through the years you have always been my biggest fan and *partner in crime.* Without your positive reinforcement and swift kicks from your velvet boot, this book would still be in the file cabinet of my mind.

Finally, to my new friend Thera: Thank you for your prayers of intercession to our heavenly Father. Clearly, they helped break up the logjam so my thoughts could flow and my fingers could fly over the keyboard to crank out my story of how God turned all my messes into messages through His saving grace.

Introduction

According to *Webster's Dictionary*, a rainbow is (1) an arc of colored light in the sky caused by refraction of the sun's rays or (2) an illusory hope and is commonly recognized when it appears in the sky, usually after it rains. My definition is quite different.

I see a rainbow as symbolic of the roads over which we travel during the course of our lifetime. Roads translate into life experiences. Life experiences come in varying tones of color—likened to the green, blue, red, and yellow colors in a rainbow that God's divine paintbrush splashes across the sky. Sometimes, our life experiences are easy and smooth—like riding on an asphalt-covered road that is perfectly level, akin to the calming colors of green and blue in the rainbow. Other times, life experiences are stony, hard, and jolting—like riding on a gravel or chip-seal road that is bumpy—comparable to high-energy colors like red and yellow. Choices are made during each experience that we have—whether good, bad, ugly, or indifferent; there are always prices paid, and they are called consequences.

Oh! Jesus moments are those times of pause (and celebration) in your life for every emotion you've experienced from the choices you've made—whether moments of joy, anger, love, hate, happiness, sadness, fear, anxiety, courage, hope, terror, guilt, grief, despair, or surprise. Regardless of the paths we take, our God-given *free will* is the tool that determines how we navigate over those roads of each life experience.

My life, although not an easy one, is probably not much different than yours. The choices you and I have made were purely and simply dictated by a little thing called *free will*. Our consequences may vary by one degree or another, but a price is paid for our choices. Mine brought me experiences that evoked two simple emotions, pain and pleasure. You see, there was a *divine constant* in my life that kept me through it all, and my strong connection to God and the Holy Spirit is what I held on to. So for every step I've taken over the green, blue, red, and yellow roads of *my rainbow*, I have some remarkable stories to tell that are filled with many *Oh! Jesus* moments.

As you read these snapshots from my life's story, you will laugh, cry, and cheer for me because you too may also personally relate to some of my experiences. Moreover, you will realize that overcoming *anything* starts in the mind.

So as you take this journey with me through the pages of my book, embrace the sanctity of life, celebrate every difficult time that you weren't sure how you'd survive—but you did—and, perhaps, *rethink* what's important in your life. You may also experience a heightened awareness and appreciation of some of your *Oh! Jesus* moments, and rediscover just how special you really are on this precious trip called *Life*.

And in case you've gotten stuck on the hump of your rainbow, my story just might help *you* get unstuck.

Section I

The Green Road

*The **purpose** of life is a life of purpose.*
Robert Byrne (1928-)

Nothing *just* happens. Each of us has a purpose to our life. I know I was born to make a difference—and so were you. During my early years, I learned that things are not always as they seem, and how we start does not determine how we finish.

1

My Beginning

*Her birth was of the womb of morning dew
and her conception of the joyous prime.*

—Edmund Spenser, *The Faerie Queene*

My rainbow began on October 2, 1945. That was the day I was conceived, and according to what my mother told me, here is how the story goes.

Mom said it was a fabulous autumn day in Baltimore to make a baby. Outside, it was seventy-one degrees; the wind was crisp, cool, and blew constantly into her windows. Three hours of morning showers gave the porch flowers a much-needed drink. Because rain usually stirred my mother's loins and caused her hormones to rage, Mom found herself wishing privately that my Dad would soon come home from work to settle her down, so to speak.

The day passed quickly, and Dad got home from work at his usual time, seven o'clock. After eating a quick dinner, Mom put my nine-month-old sister to bed and convinced Dad they should turn in early that night. After sixteen years of marriage, Mom said she knew exactly what signals to send Dad for him to know that it was definitely a *yes* night. As they lay naked on their rickety double bed while that crisp October wind blew coolly through their window, Mom gently squeezed Dad's hand—he instinctively knew what that meant—and before the fireworks started, she sweetly said, "Honey, let's make another baby tonight."

Dad gave Mom a quick grunt of agreement and proceeded to handle his business. As Dee slept peacefully in her crib, Dad's sperm did the egg dance with Mom, and by her account, fireworks flew as they did the horizontal hula that night. Mom said she knew, without a doubt, she had gotten pregnant *that night* with me. Before she fell off to sleep, she muttered to Dad that this child would also be born at home under Ms. Maggie's watchful eyes. (Maggie was the midwife who helped with my sister's birth.)

Amazingly, nine months and seven days after that October night, my mother went into labor very early Tuesday morning, July 9, 1946. As her labor pains grew more intense, Mom said her anxiety heightened about my imminent birth; and a dozen things raced through her head of stuff she needed to get done around the house—like washing the kitchen curtains, rearranging the living room furniture, and defrosting the refrigerator. But there was a slight problem. Mom only wanted to give birth with my Dad by her side. And since he was at work and not due home for about ten more hours, she came up with a plan.

> *My mother actually believed she purposefully delayed the progression of her labor pains with me by sitting down in a hard chair for an extended period of time to slow up my birth. And when she wanted to speed up her contractions to make the birth move along faster, she believed walking briskly would make that happen.*

So at 5:00 PM, a couple hours before Dad was due to come home, Mom began walking up and down the long hallway in our house to speed up those contractions. Imagine that!

As I was cranking and turning inside her belly, Mom said she began thinking about the distinct differences between her other four births. (She had given birth to three children from another marriage before she met my Dad.) I was her seventh pregnancy—two others ended in miscarriages. She went on to say she wondered if there is a correlation between the degree of birth pain and temperament of the child. Her first three births were really hard, and my two half brothers and half sister were difficult and troubled souls. With my sister Dee, Mom said the pains were smooth and easy; and Dee was an even-tempered, sweet, and docile little girl. Mom firmly believed Dee's temperament was very much connected in some way to the easy time she had in giving birth to her. *And guess what? Dee grew up to be just like that—sweet, docile, and even-tempered!*

However, the birth experience with me was quite different because I really put Mom through some paces! *And you guessed it. I was a far cry from being docile, even-tempered, and sweet.*

Mom considered herself somewhat of an expert on the process of giving birth as her labor slowly progressed into the day. Despite the warnings from Maggie, Mom was determined to wait until Dad got home from work before she pushed me out of her. Dad was there for the birth of my sister, and he definitely wouldn't miss my arrival. Privately, he hoped I would be a boy. Both Dee and I had a small audience present at our births; aunt Minnie was there for Dee's birth and aunt Juanita was there for mine.

Mom said when she glanced at the clock at 7:10 PM, she heard the jingle of Dad's keys in the front door. She continued walking up and down the long hallway in their modest two-story dwelling so her labor pains would become closer together. She could feel her body getting ready to expel me. Around 9:30 PM, after four hours of continuous walking, Mom wobbled back to her bed and asked Maggie to tell Paisley it was time; and he should come upstairs right away.

Dad skipped two steps at a time up to their second-floor bedroom. He began to comfort Mom as she pushed and waited. Finally, around five till ten, Mom asked Dad to help her get out of bed so she could stand straight up. She put her arms around Daddy's neck, straddled her legs, announced that the baby was coming, and told Maggie to get ready! Mom said she pushed really hard one last time. *Whammo!* Out I came! Now when my sister was born, the very same way, aunt Minnie called out and said, "Here comes Page-ja-lee" (that's how she pronounced my Dad's name). Aunt

Minnie said that because she believed Dee looked like my Dad. When I dropped out, my aunt Juanita told my mother to name me after her because my face was round just like hers. That's how I got my middle name, Vuanita.

The tenseness in the room suddenly lifted once I cried and began to move. My birth certificate says I was born at exactly 10:00 PM and weighed seven pounds. Mom said my face was round as a plate, and my eyes were blue as a North Carolina sky. Maggie said there was a compelling aura about my little face. I was named Vee. As Maggie cleaned me up, checking that I had all my fingers and toes, she commented to my mother how much longer it took this daughter to be born than their first girl. Being a superstitious old woman, Maggie told Mom that she felt her second daughter would be a real handful, nothing like sweet little Dee.

After the excitement over my birth subsided, Mom said she was ready for a nap. But just before falling off to sleep, she looked over at my Dad as he held me and said, "Paisley, something tells me that *this* little person is gonna be a real pistol after the hard time I just had getting her here!"

And that, my friend, was the beginning of my rainbow.

2

Sisters

*For there is no friend like a sister, in calm or stormy weather,
to cheer one on the tedious way, to fetch one if one goes astray,
to lift one if one totters down, to strengthen whilst one stands.*

—Christina Rossetti, "Goblin Market" conclusion

Dee and I were quite a handful for our forty-one-year-old mother. We were very beautiful babies with large round persuasive eyes. Dee's eyes were deep brown, sparkling, and very gentle while my eyes were sky blue, big, and inquisitive. Although we were eighteen months apart in age, we looked like twins, and Mom often dressed us alike.

Mom and Dad had been married to each other for sixteen years when Dee was born. It was a second marriage for both of them. Mom was forty years old, into early menopause, and insisted on having more children. Despite the physical limits that motherhood carried with it for a forty-year-old, our mother did not compromise on the care she provided to Dee and me. Many nights, Mom would be tired from the daily rigors of caring for two toddlers. I was especially exhausting for her because I was a rambunctious busybody while Dee was an obedient, sweet, and absolutely perfect child. Mom admitted there were times when she felt like taking a running leap to the doorway of the nursery and pitching me right into my crib at the end of the day. I regularly worked my mother's last nerve. Somehow, there was a bit of justice in having one docile daughter as a balance against a not-so-docile one. In other words, I was a tiny terror.

Dee walked at nine months, and I walked at ten months. As our little personalities blossomed and became more defined, it was clear that Dee and I were exact opposites. I took on assertive characteristics while Dee assumed more passive and gentle characteristics. From the moment I could speak in sentences, I was mouthy. Dee, on the other hand, was an observant and cooperative child.

As we grew up, we were like second skins to each other. Ours was an inseparable bond. Even though I was always referred to as the baby, I was very protective of my older sister. As little girls, we were affectionately labeled Lady and Loosie. Dee was the shy and modestly quiet one called Lady. While I was a brazen and outspoken little person, I was called Loosie.

When it came to school, Dee was the scholar, easily excelling. I would only learn when my curiosity was stirred. Even as a child, I had my mother's disposition and a lot of her characteristics: charming, controlling, manipulative, charismatic, and savvy. Dee had Dad's—even-tempered, intelligent, patient, tolerant, soft-spoken, and unassuming.

Because our parents were older and very firm disciplinarians, they were not as inclined to let us go out to play quite as much as other kids were allowed by their parents. Instead, we were made to study our schoolwork and Sunday school lessons. Dee was always the diligent one when it came to getting homework lessons completed. I usually required a quick swat or two from the strap to help me settle down so I could finish my homework.

My mother was a staunch Baptist who took us to Sunday school and church every week. Daddy generally stayed home and prepared Sunday dinners, which were usually chicken and dumplings. Dad was a great cook, except for making biscuits. Although Dad was a chef for a rural hospital early in his career, he never could make good biscuits. Whenever he did bake them, they were always really hard like hockey pucks, so Dad left the task of making biscuits up to Mom; hers were always soft and perfect—even a day or two later, they were amazingly still soft. (Mom showed me many times how she made her biscuits, but I never quite got the hang of it.)

Mom fancied herself as a teacher or sorts. When Dee was five and a half years old and I was four, our mother began writing recitations for us to memorize and publicly recite in Sunday school. Some of those recitations were really long, but our mother took great pains in teaching us to publicly speak to church audiences. Although Mom was very poised, soft-spoken, and eloquent, she could be very demanding and would not hesitate to swat our legs with a switch whenever we missed words from memory. Giving us praise and encouragement for doing a good job or loving hugs of affection were not a part of my mother's personality. (I didn't learn how valuable hugs were until I became an adult.)

As additional practice for us to improve our diction, Mom made Dee and me sit in a chair in front of her, usually while she was ironing, and read books to her. Oftentimes, I would start to squirm and beg to stop reading so I could go out to play, but Mom cut me no slack. At four years old, I constantly tried to fool my mother during my reading assignments. As I would read aloud to her, I would mix up the words and leave some of them out in my haste to finish the task. But somehow, Mom always heard the mistakes I made and demanded that I reread those pages! Under my breath, I would mumble how I couldn't understand how she knew what the page said since I was the one holding the book! But invariably, her ears always caught the errors, and I could never fool her. (To my amazement when I became a parent, I also gave my daughter reading assignments like my mom did for me. I recognized I had that same ability to hear missed and dropped words when she read to me. And needless to say, my daughter also wondered how I knew when she left out words because she was holding the book!)

Mom enjoyed the praise she received from her church friends on how cute her little girls looked while standing on top of the offering table, reciting the jingles and short stories she made us memorize. Our recitations were funny as well as inspirational.

When Dee gave her speeches, her style was graceful, ladylike, and gentle. Her sparkling brown eyes and well-timed curtsy after her recitations would always result in overwhelming applause. At the Sunday school Christmas program in 1952, Dee spoke about Mary, Joseph, and baby Jesus. The crowded church gave her a standing ovation. She was terrific! My sister was a *natural* when it came to learning stuff. I, on the other hand, required lots of *corporal* prodding.

I had a different type of delivery when I recited. I was a real ham for the attention I received. So when I spoke in church, I did more entertaining for the audience—by my gestures and in the way I expressed myself—than inspiring them with my little talks. Most of the time, the church would let out rip-roaring laughter in response to my antics. I was quickly labeled as *that funny little one.*

3

Tiny Terror

Boys will be boys—and even that . . . wouldn't matter if we could only prevent girls from being girls.

—Anthony Hope (1863-1933)

Once Dee and I started school, my parents regularly received notes from my teachers about my behavior. We attended the same elementary school; and because Dee was a bright and studious child, she was allowed to go straight into first grade, skipping kindergarten. She was a joy for all her teachers. Early school experiences for me, however, were somewhat different.

I shall never forget my first day in kindergarten. It was quite eventful, to say the least. There weren't enough chairs for all the kids to sit in. So I sauntered over to a little boy named Russell (the dirtiest boy in the class), made friends with him, and innocently sat on his lap. At that time, I wasn't exactly sure why the teacher became so upset with me for doing that, but I was not about to sit on the floor in the nicely pressed dress Mom had put on me that morning. The teacher quickly made me get off Russell's lap. She never explained to me why it was not a nice thing that I had done. Instead, she wrote a note to my parents. Since my teacher knew Dee was my older sister in the class next door, she gave her the note to take home to our parents. I guess my teacher knew I wouldn't deliver it.

After reading the teacher's note, both Mom and Dad were very upset with me. Daddy told Mom to handle that matter with me. Mama told me I was "fresh," and if I didn't watch myself, I would get in a lot of trouble as a fast-tail little girl. At five years old, I had no clue what a *fast-tail* little girl was, much less what Mom meant by calling me *fresh*. I was just being friendly to Russell!

The years that followed my first day in kindergarten were quite normal for a kid who was the little terror that I was. When things were dull, I would think up mischief for Dee and me to get into. We were often mistaken as twins. If you saw one of us, you would see the other close by. As children, we mostly lived in row houses in the inner city of Baltimore. Although our family moved, what seemed like every year, I could always find activities to make playtime fun. Dee trusted me and, most times, enjoyed the risks I'd influence her to take with me. Time after time, she followed me into mischief despite the penalties we paid in the name of fun. But there were times I'd play by myself when I couldn't convince her to join me. Like the time I wanted to throw mud pies onto a mean neighbor's front door and Dee didn't. And, of course, being the level-headed sister, she insisted that I shouldn't throw those pies. Or when I scared the kids in the block chasing them through our back alley, dangling a dead mouse by its tail. Dee ran away from me just like the other kids! She hated mice, but there was very little that frightened me.

One of the dumbest things I ever did was when I accepted a dare from my little friends in the neighborhood. One of the houses we lived in had a small window in the middle of a double staircase. I opened the window and taunted the kids who were standing below me in the alley. They dared me to jump out of that window. And like a nut, I did. When I hit the cement pavement, I landed in a squatting position. Let me just tell you, *that* was truly an *Oh! Jesus* moment. The pain that shot up my leg into my hip was excruciating. I slowly stood up, limped around for a few days, and didn't think much about the incident anymore. In my mind, I was brave for taking the dare. (Little did I know that little stunt would physically and painfully plague me later in my life.)

My favorite mischief was naptime capers. During the summer while school was out, Mom would make us take an afternoon nap. Instead of taking a nap, I would convince Dee to join me in whatever notion of fun that popped into my head. Most times, when I'd share a fun idea with her (except for the mouse game), she was agreeable to my suggestion. Other times, when she wasn't convinced what I was suggesting would be fun, she would always ask me the same question: "Are you *sure* we won't get in trouble?"

And my reply was usually convincing, "Nah, we won't get caught. You'll see."

One particular hot summer day in 1954, I convinced Dee that instead of taking a nap, we should get out of bed and run up and down the porch roofs to cool ourselves off. (The neighborhood we lived in had overhanging roofs over each back porch, making a perfect runway.) This exercise soon became our favorite. Usually, we could run over those overhangs without getting caught. We would skip, run up and down those rooftops, make lots of noise, giggle loudly, and have ourselves a high time. For a while, no one saw us nor told our mother. However, that caper was short-lived because someone *did* see us and told Mom. One day, as we were running back to our bedroom window to get back in bed for our nap, I saw my mother's head sticking out of the window looking at us. She wasn't smiling and looked really upset. That was another *Oh! Jesus* moment. I knew we were in big trouble. Suddenly, I felt sick to my stomach because Mom had caught me misbehaving again, and there was no question in her mind as to who started the mischief. But I felt sicker at the thought that Dee was also in trouble because of me. After Mom beat our butts, we cried ourselves to sleep from the spanking for our antics.

I used to believe that my mother had built-in radar to know exactly when to catch me misbehaving. Somehow, she could suddenly appear at the right moment and catch me red-handed when I was doing something I had no business doing. Like the time I tried to learn how to smoke cigarettes when I was supposed to be taking my afternoon nap.

Mom made extra money by renting out rooms in our house to boarders. One boarder in particular, Mr. Spencer, smoked cigarettes and would leave the butts in ashtrays in his room. Smoking looked fascinating, and I wanted to see for myself how to do it. So one afternoon while Mr. Spencer was at work, I snuck into his room, took one of the used cigarette butts out of an ashtray, and rambled through his nightstand to find myself a match to light the cigarette. After I had rounded up what I needed to try my hand at smoking, I quietly crept back to my room, opened the window so the smoke could escape once I lit the cigarette, put it in my mouth, and imitated the way I saw Mr. Spencer smoke his cigarettes. It didn't take long before I had the hang of how not to choke on the smoke. I discovered I didn't like the way it tasted. But at the very moment I was making up my mind not to smoke it anymore, my mother burst through the door and caught me with that cigarette butt in my little hand. The suddenness of her opening the door startled me, and I began choking on the smoke. I saw the strap in Mama's hand, and the next thing I knew, she had turned me across her knees and was pounding away on my rear end. It felt like she was trying to kill me with those hard licks. For sure, getting caught red-handed with that cigarette was another *Oh! Jesus* moment.

I guess the spanking Mom gave me was her way of discouraging me from trying that stunt again. When she finally let me up, she told me I had more of the same coming when my Dad got home. Fortunately, my sister was not a part of this adventure and didn't get a spanking. I was real happy about that.

From that day on, I have never had any interest in smoking cigarettes. But later that year, my life temporarily took a different turn when I met my mother's best friend.

4

The Great Introduction

Gentle Jesus, meek and mild
Look upon a little child,
Pity my simplicity, suffer me to come to Thee

—Charles Wesley, "Gentle Jesus"

My mother was a very religious woman. To me, it seemed like she listened to just about every radio preacher in the world. Oliver B. Green was her weekday favorite. She also attended church every Sunday and other church services during the week when she was able. In the fall of 1954, one of her favorite evangelists, Oral Roberts, came to town for a revival. Mom was beside herself with joy.

The Saturday morning the revival began, Mom told me I was going with her. Dee said she had a headache, so she didn't have to go with Mom and me to the service. (Dee discovered if she faked having a headache, she could get out of being dragged to church.) Mom and Dad were very compassionate to my sister when it came to her headaches. Whenever Dee said her head hurt, I was the one left who had to go with Mom to her different church services, whether I wanted to or not. I figured because I was the one who misbehaved most of the time, Mom wanted to keep a watchful eye on me. Dad didn't go to church, so asking him to go was out of the question. Instead, I learned to just hush and do what I was told.

On that crisp fall Saturday, Mom and I caught the trolley car around noon to go to Edmondson Village for the big revival. As we were riding along, I began complaining about having to go to church again. I asked my mother why I couldn't stay home like Dee. Mom looked at me with her piercing eyes and said, "*Cause you're gonna meet Mr. Jesus.*" Mom's answer confused me. I wasn't exactly sure who Mr. Jesus was or why I had to meet him. Suddenly, I felt a little frightened.

I sat there for a moment as the trolley chugged along on its way and thought to myself, *Could this be the same Mr. Jesus that Dee and I have heard Mama calling out to late at night when she and Dad were supposed to be sleeping? Or was he somebody different?* Mom saw the curious look on my face and told me that Dee would also be with us had it not been for her headache. She went on to say, "Once you meet Mr. Jesus, child, you will have a friend for life! He is someone you can share all your secrets with. He will never tell anyone what you tell him. And whether you know it or not, Jesus loves you very much regardless of how naughty you act or even how good you try to be."

After she said that, I didn't feel frightened anymore, so I settled down and waited for the trolley car to arrive at the revival. As we approached our stop, I could see a great big tent. All I could think about at that moment was how much the tent reminded me of the circus and wished Dee was with me. I didn't know what to expect, so I stayed close to Mom as we walked inside the big tent. Seeing so many people in that tent was quite a sight for an eight-year-old. Mom and I quickly found ourselves a nice seat close to the front of the stage.

The music was so beautiful, the people were very friendly, and everyone seemed to be having a good time. Mr. Roberts began preaching. I don't remember the title of his sermon, but I do remember his excitement when he shouted out to the audience, "Jesus is in this place!" I quickly turned around so I could get a look at him for myself, but I didn't see anyone special. Oral Robert then asked everyone who didn't know Jesus to stand up. I looked at my Mom; she nodded that it was okay for me to stand up to meet Mr. Jesus. A lot of other people also stood up.

Next I was shuffled along with a good-size group of people, including other kids like me, into a smaller tent. The floor of the tent was covered with woodchips and sawdust. There were chairs placed in a circle, and we were told to have a seat. I was fascinated by all the excitement around me, and I remember thinking to myself how special Mr. Jesus must be for everyone to be making such a fuss over us.

A very kind older lady spoke to us as we were seated in the circle. She said some of the same things Mama told me on the bus. I figured she and Mama must be friends because she also knew that Mr. Jesus didn't tell our secrets. Then the lady asked us, "Do you want to go to heaven?" I had heard Mama talk about heaven lots of times, so I raised my hand because I thought heaven would be a nice place to visit. She told us, in great detail, about something called the plan of salvation and the story of who Jesus Christ is.

She began her incredible story by saying that Jesus Christ is the son of God. She went on to tell us about a magical thing God did of splitting himself into a flesh and blood person and a spirit person. He then sent the flesh and blood part of himself to earth in human form as a baby. This baby was born at Christmas to an earthly mother and father by the names of Mary and Joseph. They named their baby Jesus Christ. The more she told us about the arrival of Jesus, my interest in what she was saying grew stronger and stronger, and I did not squirm or get restless.

In my little mind, I compared the arrival of Jesus Christ to the earth very much like the arrival of Superman. Jesus came in the form of a brand-new baby, and folklore says Superman, as a toddler, dropped out of the sky in a little spaceship onto earth. When Superman came to planet earth, his mission was to help rid the world of bad guys. But when Jesus came to earth, his mission was to serve mankind and save us from our sins once we believe in our hearts that Christ is the way for us to go to heaven when we die.

The lady continued telling the story of when Jesus was thirty-three years old, how Roman soldiers killed him because he told people in the town that he *was* the son of God. That statement angered the elders and chief priests, so the Roman soldiers crucified Jesus by nailing him to a cross. He hung on that cross, enduring physical torture from the soldiers for about six hours as well as taunts and ridicule from the massive crowd who was watching all this. Finally, Jesus cried out to his father, "Into thine hands I commit my Spirit." And then he died. The soldiers took him down from the cross, put his body in a special place called a tomb, and rolled a big stone in front of the tomb to keep Jesus from getting out because he had announced that he would rise from the dead in three days. And magically, just as he predicted, Jesus did come back to life and walked out of the tomb after three days.

She went on to tell us that after Jesus had visited with a few of his friends and family, he miraculously ascended up into the sky to rejoin his father,

God, as the Bible states in John 16:28 (I came forth from the Father, and am come into the world: again, I leave the world, and go to the Father). Then the lady said that each of us who believed that Jesus lived and died for us would go to the happy place when we died called heaven. Although I didn't know very much about dying, I was sure that I didn't want to take a chance of not believing there is a place called heaven. I knew I wanted to go to the happy place.

The most exciting part of her story was once I accepted and believed in the existence of God, his son, Jesus, and his Holy Spirit, she told me that God's spirit would live inside of my heart and comfort me in times of trouble from that day forward!

After she finished speaking to the group in the small tent, we were given Bibles, instructed to turn to a book called John, and told to follow along with her as she read the scripture John 3:16: "For God so loved the world, that he gave his only begotten Son, that whosoever believeth in him should not perish, but have everlasting life."

Even though I was only eight years old, I knew I wanted Jesus Christ as my special friend just like Mama said. So I knelt down in the floor covered with woodchips and sawdust, bowed my head, and spoke to God from the bottom of my heart. I said,

> Oh God, I am a sinner. I believe Jesus is your son and that he died on a cross just for me. I also believe His shed blood, death, burial, and resurrection was the price paid for my soul. I now receive, by faith, Jesus Christ as my savior. I thank you, Lord, for forgiving me of my sins and all the bad things I have done like getting my sister in trouble, talking back to my parents, and not telling the truth all the time. I thank you for the gift of salvation and everlasting life because of your merciful grace. I want you to come and live in my heart and be my best friend. Amen.

After I finished praying, I felt a warm feeling of comfort cover me in a way that I cannot describe. I also learned that once Jesus ascended back to heaven, he no longer was a flesh and blood person, but a spirit. At that moment, I began thinking of Jesus Christ as my invisible friend.

When prayer time was over, we were told that we were now "saved." (Being *saved* is the term used to describe ones life after they seek God's forgiveness for their sins and consciously ask Jesus Christ into their life as their Savior). I felt so happy about what had just happened to me and skipped out of that tent to find my mother. When I found her, I was full of laughter. I showed Mom my Bible and told her what I had just learned about God, His son, Jesus Christ, and the Holy Spirit. Mama had tears in her eyes when she smiled at me and softly said, "Vee, now that you've asked Jesus to be *your* friend, your life will *never* be the same."

Following that autumn day at the Oral Roberts revival, my new friendship with Mr. Jesus was tested many times.

5

My Best Friend

*Acquaintance I would have, but when't depends
not on the number, but the choice of friends.*

—Abraham Cowley (1618-1667)

It was late and very dark outside as Mom and I rode the trolley car back home from the Oral Roberts revival. The revival had lasted all day, and I was tired and sleepy from all the excitement, so I laid my head on Mama's lap and went to sleep.

It felt like I had just closed my eyes when Mom woke me up to tell me we had reached our stop and had to get off the trolley. As I stumbled along the street where we lived, waking up enough to start chattering, I began telling my mother about some of the interesting things I had learned about Jesus. As we walked along, I asked Mom why Jesus was a spirit instead of a real person. I told her how I didn't like the idea of talking to a spirit and that I really wanted to see Jesus with my own two eyes. Although Mama listened to me, she never answered my questions. We finally reached our front door, and Mom was anxious to get indoors so we both could go to bed.

But just before I got into bed, Mama said, "Now that Jesus is in your heart, Vee, you will soon start to know that his friendship is very real even though you can't see him with your own two eyes. But you will feel Him. So for now, you should simply think of him as your invisible friend."

That next day while Dee and I were getting ready for Sunday school, I couldn't stop talking about what happened to me at the revival the day before. I told her all about my new invisible friend named Jesus. She didn't say anything when I told her she would also have been introduced to Mr. Jesus if she hadn't gotten a headache.

Mama knew a lot about Jesus and talked about Him, seemingly, all the time. During my childhood, I remember my mother having many *Oh! Jesus* moments. I didn't understand why she used the *Oh! Jesus* exclamation as much as she did, but she used the expression so much until Dee and I just came to expect to hear it regularly in our house. If Mom stomped her toe or hurt herself doing chores around the house, she would always say *Oh! Jesus*. Whenever she shouted in church, Dee and I could hear her from across the room crying out, "*Oh! Jesus!*" Although our parents slept in separate bedrooms, it was normal on some nights for us to hear Mom's *Oh! Jesus* outcries from Daddy's room. The way I figured it, Jesus was real special for him to be the person Mom called on in times of excitement. *Oh! Jesus* were her two favorite words.

Particularly after I became a believer in Jesus Christ, Mom made sure Dee and I went to Sunday school every week. We didn't like getting up early on Sunday morning for more school, but after attending a few classes, I realized I really liked Sunday school a lot. As I learned more Bible stories, I grew to value my new friendship with Jesus and soon discovered that I really loved Old Testament stories. David and Solomon quickly became my two favorite people in the Bible. Although David was a real rascal who got into a lot of trouble a few times, I liked him because he was brave, and I liked Solomon because he was a very wise man who was sought after for his ability to solve problems. So every night when I said my prayers, I would ask Jesus to make me wise like Solomon and brave like David.

The more I learned about Jesus, the more curious I grew about exactly how he could do all those miracles the Bible described. Like his first miracle at the wedding in Cana when he turned water into wine! Or like the time when he turned two fish and five loaves of bread into enough food to feed over five thousand people, and there were enough leftovers to fill up twelve baskets! That was truly an awesome miracle, and I have never understood how seven items could be divided among five thousand people, with leftovers no less! The more I read about the travels and miracles of Jesus, I became more convinced than ever that if he was truly my invisible friend, I could expect him to perform a miracle or two in my behalf.

Two significant things happened to me at age ten that caused me to finally accept the reality of my friendship with Jesus. One was my Dad standing up for me when my science teacher accused me of lying about ownership of a science project, and the second was when I became the state female hopscotch champion of Maryland.

By the time I reached the fifth grade, I had quite a reputation as a chatterbox in school. My teachers continued sending notes home to my parents asking them to encourage me to stop being disruptive and talkative in class. My mouth often got me into a lot of trouble with my teachers. Once I was suspended for talking back—and for good reason.

During fifth grade, my class was assigned a science project. Dad diligently helped me work on that assignment, and I was very proud of the finished project. It was about the solar system. Dad helped me draw the chain of circles that was a display of the planets and carefully monitored my work, making sure it was neat. I took my project to school, laid it on my desk, and walked away briefly. Another girl in my class (whose name escapes me) took my work off my desk, erased my name, and wrote hers on the front page. When I returned to my seat, I noticed my science project was missing and saw the girl holding my work. I asked her to give it back, and she said I was mistaken because *it* was her project. I immediately told my teacher what happened.

Mrs. Sturdivant didn't believe me and called the other girl up to her desk so she could get to the bottom of who was telling the truth. Apparently, she was convinced the other girl was telling the truth; and I was accused of lying, was taken to the principal's office, and sent home that day. I was suspended for something I was not guilty of—except, of course, loudly stating my case that I wasn't lying about the solar project, in fact, being mine. My feelings were hurt because no one believed me. I bawled all the way home and did a lot of talking to my best friend. That day, I learned that being a chatterbox had seriously reduced my credibility in Mrs. Sturdivant's eyes because she did not believe that the solar system project was mine.

Dad happened to have come home early from work that day and met me at the front door when I came in. He immediately asked me why I was not in school. I told him what had just happened. In his calm demeanor, Dad asked me to bring him his hat and told me to get in the car. Although I wasn't sure of what was about to happen, I knew my Dad was about to come to my defense. I felt very special as Dad drove me back to that school. I said a quick prayer asking my best friend to make everything okay. The stern look on Dad's face and his curled lip made me know he was on a mission, and it was a wonderful feeling to know my Dad had my back.

When we arrived at my school, we got out of the car. Dad took me by the hand, and we walked boldly to the principal's office. I felt very safe with my Dad by my side. Once inside, Dad stood but insisted that I sit in a chair. Because Dad's voice was clear, resonant, and sounded like God's, he was never ignored once he spoke. As he told the principal what had happened to me earlier that day, she asked him to have a seat while she summoned Mrs. Sturdivant.

My science teacher came to the principal's office and shyly greeted Dad after being introduced to him by the principal. Dad proceeded to tell Mrs. Sturdivant that he was alarmed that she accused me of lying about the science project being mine when he himself had helped me put it together, so he knew for a fact that it was mine. Then he described the project in detail to both women. Next he turned to Mrs. Sturdivant and said, "How dare you call my daughter a liar and have her suspended because you didn't bother to look into this matter more closely!" Mrs. Sturdivant's face turned redder and redder with each word Dad spoke. Finally, in his calm manner, Dad told both the principal and Mrs. Sturdivant that he wanted that situation corrected immediately and an apology be given to *his little girl* for what they had put me through.

No doubt, those two white women had never had a black man stand up to them as my Dad did that day. I was given an A on my project, the classmate who stole my work was suspended, and both the principal and Mrs. Sturdivant apologized to me for the *misunderstanding*, as they called it. That was truly an unforgettable *Oh! Jesus* moment in my life!

A saving grace for me while in elementary school was my counselor, Mr. Wallace. He helped me redirect my disruptive energies by registering me as a contestant in the local Maryland hopscotch championship.

Mr. Wallace did a lot of pleading to Mom to let me participate in that contest, not to mention the many prayers I prayed for Jesus to let her agree. I knew that because Mom expected me to come straight home from school to make Dad's pot of coffee and start dinner, she wouldn't be too keen on anything disrupting my daily chores. Briefly put, I needed a miracle! Privately, I liked the idea of the hopscotch event, even though I knew very little about it, just so I could get a break from my mother's kitchen. And guess what? Mom consented for me to participate in the hopscotch championship but made Mr. Wallace promise to personally guarantee my safety and bring me home promptly after the practice sessions.

"Thank you, Lord, for giving Mom a good attitude about me being in the contest!"

I immediately focused my thoughts on winning.

The contest was on the Monday following two full weeks of practice sessions. Even though the game of hopscotch was considered a girl's game, I competed against many boys and beat them handily. I talked to my friend Jesus a lot during the competition, asking Him to help me do a good job. After several days of throwing that rubber heel and hopping through the numbered squares, not touching the lines, I quickly defeated all the other girls who competed for the spot to represent our elementary school in the competition.

Getting my picture in the paper and bringing home the medal for being the best female hopscotch player in Maryland was a glorious day for me. I felt really special. Especially for the two weeks my school gave me free lunch as a reward for winning the girls' competition. Those hot lunches were so much better than the Velveeta cheese sandwiches Mom slathered with that nasty sandwich spread she made me take for lunch every day!

Although I wanted a hug or a pat on the back of congratulations from my parents for my accomplishment in the competition, I never let them see my disappointment when they showed no excitement for what I had done. (Affectionate hugs and encouragement from our parents were not something Dee and I experienced growing up nor did our parents ever say "I love you" to us.) Instead, I learned at a young age to encourage myself by whistling and humming whenever I did anything that I thought deserved praise. (Little did I know that the absence of encouragement and affection from my parents shaped some of my adult behavior.)

Being rewarded with hot lunches at school for two weeks sparked the notion in my head to find a way to continue buying myself hot lunches at school because I really didn't like taking bagged lunches to school. My parents could not afford to give me 35¢ every day, so I decided to find a job and make some money. As I think back to that time, my determination to find a job and earn money to buy hot lunches at school was a baby step of independence, so to speak.

I quickly found myself a Saturday job cleaning a neighbor's house since I no longer went with Dad on his Saturday grocery runs. Although I was only ten years old, I was mature for my age and quite handy with a bucket of soapy water. I began buying hot lunches at school with the $2 I had left of my pay from my weekend job. Actually, I made $4, but my mother took half of my money for herself. She said that was her cut for allowing me to have the job.

Mom bought a piano and plucked on it every now and then. Next she got the notion that I should take piano lessons and quickly located a music teacher by the name of Ms. Francis. I began taking piano lessons twice a week at Ms. Francis' house. I was quite a busy ten-year-old who now had two music lessons a week, a Saturday job, my regular schoolwork and cooking chores. Again, those piano lessons were a wonderful distraction that helped me escape going right home after school to start dinner and make Dad's coffee. *Mom cooked on those days I had commitments.* I worked really hard at my music to learn my notes, chords, and arpeggios because I wanted to be good at playing piano. Ms. Francis was very pleased with me and said I was a quick study. Once my mother noticed that I was playing melodies, she gave me a hymn book and told me to learn to play a few of those songs for her.

Mom had a very sweet but soft voice. She hummed and sang as she worked around the house—either reading her Bible, doing the laundry, ironing, or just sitting in her rocking chair looking out our big bay window in the living room. The very first hymn I learned to play was "Nearer, My God, to Thee." Mom wore me out by making me play that song over and over and over as she sang in the background. Although Mama never told me how pleased she was with my progress on the piano, I could tell she liked my music because she would regularly ask me what new hymn had I learned. So naturally, I always looked for the easiest tunes in the hymnal to play for her.

As elementary school graduation approached, Ms. Francis included me in a big piano recital. The song chosen for me to play was Moonlight Sonata by Ludwig van Beethoven. I worked really hard to play that song perfectly. Ms. Francis was very excited over my progress and told me how proud she was of how good I was playing. When the day of the recital arrived, I couldn't keep still. The thought of playing on a large stage in front of hundreds of people was a bigger thrill than winning my hopscotch medal and scary at the same time.

Just before dinner, Mom dressed me in my favorite Sunday outfit, a beautiful navy and baby blue dress with a fancy crinoline slip underneath. I looked marvelous! As I sat at the dinner table tapping my right foot in anticipation, the excitement of the recital stole my appetite, and I just couldn't eat. My mother could not (and would not) understand my anxiety but firmly kept telling me to eat my dinner. I was fidgety and nervous about the recital and just didn't want to eat my dinner. I tried to make my mother understand that I didn't have an appetite, but she told me if I didn't eat, I wouldn't go to the recital. I tried forcing something down but felt like I would throw up, so I put my fork down and just sat there. Despite her threats to keep me home from the recital if I didn't eat my dinner, I still couldn't eat. It was a war of wills between my mother and me that night. And sure enough, Mama made me take off my pretty outfit and go to bed without dinner. I cried most of the night and, for the first time, fussed with Jesus, asking Him why he didn't rescue me. Eventually, I fell off to sleep.

It was a long time after that before I forgave my mother for taking that opportunity away from me of making me miss that recital. After my musical disappointment, I lost interest in playing piano and eventually stopped taking music lessons from Ms. Francis.

I never had another chance to play in a recital after that nor have I ever played the Moonlight Sonata since.

6

First Steps of Liberty

I must have liberty—withal, as large a charter as the wind,
to blow on whom I please.

—Shakespeare

After my sixth-grade graduation and at the end of that summer, to make extra money, Mom rented out a spare bedroom in our house to Cousin Nezzie who was starting college that fall. One day, as I passed by her room, I spotted a big contraption sitting on her table; and my curiosity got the best of me. So I went into her room and asked if I could take a closer look; it was a typewriter.

Nezzie explained how the typewriter worked and asked me if I wanted to give it a try, cautioning me to be very careful not to hit the keys too hard. She gently placed my two hands on the keyboard—what she called the home row—and started teaching me how to type four of the ten alphabets on the home row. I quickly got the hang of typing *D* and *F* with the left hand and *J* and *K* with the right hand. First, I lightly tapped each key; then I got faster and could type those four letters really fast even with my eyes closed.

Piles of papers fascinated me. I loved to tinker with papers, sorting them and making different piles of junk papers. Mama used to say to me, "You have more papers around this house than a Philadelphia lawyer!" My love for papers and the typewriter caused me to start thinking about what I wanted to be when I grew up. Deep down inside, I knew I'd be something connected to an office, a typewriter and especially the written word. By the time I entered junior high school, I knew typing was definitely a class I would enjoy.

Junior high school was an exciting new adventure for me. I especially loved going to a different room for the classes I took. It didn't take me very long to pick out a cute boy as incentive to make going to school more interesting. His name was Michael. It was a silent attraction on my part and definitely one-sided because Michael seemingly only talked at length with nice looking girls. He never noticed me because I wasn't cute, but rather homely looking. Despite that, I eagerly got up for school each morning and watched him strut through the halls when classes changed.

I wasn't the type of student who enjoyed subjects like math, geography, and science; but I did enjoy English and music. Initially, my primary interest was in home economics and later English. I became a terrific speller and won a spelling bee in my second year of junior high. Since home economics didn't require too much use of my brain, I managed to do well in that class. My love for music was still deep inside of me, so I signed up to be in the school choir. Although I didn't play the piano at that time, knowing how to read music was a big help in holding tones.

On the days I had after-school activities to attend, Mom would cook, and it generally was very good because she was, in fact, a great cook. Except those times when she fixed us that stinky kidney stew. Otherwise, dinnertime was great because our family sat at the kitchen table together. I guess having the cooking responsibility so early in my life was Mom's way of equipping me to be a housekeeper and mother someday—although I couldn't see it then.

As far as Dee picking up my slack and starting dinner on those occasions when I would be late, that did not happen. Mom insisted that Dee come home from school and "get her studyin' done." It was no secret that I was not studious like my sister, and Mom reminded me of that fact often.

As I walked home one hot spring day toward the end of my first year of junior high, I came upon a church in the middle of the block that caught my attention for some odd reason. It was right around the corner from where we lived. I decided to visit that church and told Mom I would not be going to church with her that Sunday. She said okay. I guess Mom didn't give me a hard time about not going to her church because I would still be going to services. Attending church on Sunday was an absolute in our house.

I enjoyed the lively and spirited services at the new church and visited it several times during the spring and into summer. On one of my Sunday morning visits, I happened to stay after service to check out a youth trip that was announced in the church bulletin. The meeting was held in the Sunday school auditorium. The room was full of young teens like me. I sat on the piano bench. After the meeting was over, I twirled around on the bench and began playing a hymn from the hymnal lying on the piano. *Although it had been quite a while since I had played piano, I could still read music.* One of the older deacons came over to me and excitedly said, "Gurl, (like old folk would say) you play nice. We need a church organist, and I think you'd do good!"

The deacon went on to mention that the job paid $40 a month, and each Sunday, I would accompany the church pianist during the morning service. Mr. Brown was an awesome piano player, and I was very excited to team up with such a talented musician. When Mr. Brown played the piano, he sounded like a nickelodeon master. Although I didn't say yes to Deacon Gist on the spot, I knew in my heart I definitely wanted the job but I had to work out some details in my head!

The invitation to be the church organist was a wonderful *Oh! Jesus* moment. Being offered that job rekindled my interest in music. Aside from earning a lot of money, I could possibly learn to play better music with Mr. Brown as my mentor. I also knew if I accepted the job, I would have to stand up to my mother when I told her I'd no longer be going with her to church. I really didn't enjoy my mother's boring church services as much as I did the service at Friendship Baptist.

As I walked home from Friendship that Sunday, I made up my mind I definitely wanted to take the organist job, so I began talking to my friend Jesus about the situation. I wasn't exactly sure how Mom would react when she learned I wanted to leave her church and play the organ at another church, but all the way home, I asked Jesus to pull some heavenly strings and not let Mom get angry about what I wanted to do when I broke the news to her. And I told Jesus I was no longer willing to give up half of my pay each month to my mother and asked him to fix that also. It would take a miracle to soften Mom's heart. For this opportunity, I was willing to stand my ground and take my first real steps of liberty.

I waited until my family was eating dinner that Sunday afternoon before I brought up the matter about my job offer at Friendship. After taking two or three bites of my mashed potatoes, I took a quick gulp of water to wet my throat. I nervously blurted out that I was asked to play the organ for Friendship Baptist. I went on to say that I was excited about the opportunity and wanted to accept the job. After I boldly stated my case, silence followed at the dinner table.

My mother's first reaction was a grunt. Dad continued to eat and didn't say anything or even look up from his plate. Next I announced that I wanted to become a member of Friendship Baptist. I ended my announcement by telling my mother I no longer would be attending church with her and hoped she wouldn't be too upset about my decision. I respectfully stated how important this opportunity was to me. Then I shut up and waited for a response.

After a moment or two, it was obvious to me that Mom wasn't upset over my news. She finally spoke and said, "That will be nice, Vee." I almost fell out of my chair with shock! This truly was answered prayer. My friend Jesus had pulled his heavenly strings and worked this situation out perfectly for me. Changing Mom's mind was truly a miracle. I felt so special to have Jesus as my friend! (In retrospect, a small part of me believed that Mom let me take the organist job as amends for not letting me participate in my sixth-grade piano recital.)

It was around this time in my life that I started hearing one specific scripture in my head from time to time, Matthew 5:13: "Ye are the salt of the earth: but if the salt have lost his savor, wherewith shall it be salted? It is thenceforth good for nothing, but to be cast out, and to be trodden under foot of men." (KJV) At first, I really didn't have a clue what this scripture meant. (I realized much later in my life that God was telling me, through His Word, that I had the opportunity through my life and testimony to bring blessing to others.)

My first choir rehearsal was two days later. I had never been up close to an organ, and I certainly didn't know what to do with one. Nevertheless, I nervously climbed onto the organ bench, checked out all the buttons, put my feet on those big pedals, and somehow played my first hymn along with Mr. Brown. For me to be untrained on that large music machine, it was purely God's grace that enabled me to make magical sounds come out of that organ every Sunday, playing alongside Mr. Brown. Ours was a match made in heaven. From the night of my first rehearsal up until I left Friendship five years later, Mr. Brown and I rocked that church to the rafters praising God on our keyboards!

I have learned that . . .

- **Children are divine gifts from God.**

    1. Children need us to CHERISH every minute with them.
    2. Children need us to HUG them *so they know they are important to us.*
    3. Children need us to SHOW INTEREST in what they do *because they want our approval.*
    4. Children need us to LISTEN to what they say *because they are worthy of our attention.*

- **All kids need a little help, a little hope, and somebody who believes in them.**

    1. Children need us to RESPECT them *because this is how they learn to care about others.*
    2. Children need us to ENCOURAGE them *because this is how they become the best that they can.*
    3. Children need us to NURTURE them *because the world can be a harsh place.*
    4. Children need our verbal interaction *so they can learn to be communicators.*

Section II

The Blue Road

Experience is a hard teacher.
She gives the test first and the lessons afterwards.

Anonymous

I came to the frightening conclusion that when I was born, "woe" should have been my middle name. There were so many hard lessons that brought me much pain. However, the next span of my life reached heights and depths unimaginable. I embraced my pain as information, not punishment, and made it the lamp of experience by which my feet are directed.

7

My First Storm

*The storm has gone over me; and I lie like one of those old oaks
which the late hurricane has scattered about me.
I am striped of all my honours; I am torn up by the roots,
and lie prostrate on the earth!*

—Edmund Burke (1729-1797)

Playing the organ at church helped me with my typing skills. Although the keyboards were different, finger dexterity on the typewriter was important and came easier for me the more my fingers slid over the organ's keyboard. Each semester in my junior high typing classes got better and better. I received several certificates of merit for my progress, and by the time I graduated junior high, I was typing a cool forty-five words a minute with only five errors on a ten-minute timed test. My last report card clearly indicated I enjoyed English, home economics, and typing much more than math, geography, and French. With high school as my next step, improving on my typing was a top priority for me.

Before I started high school, the summer of 1961 was quite eventful. First, I developed a strong interest in radio broadcasting; and second, I found a job as a live-in housekeeper and nanny of sorts. My job as a domestic paid me $35 a week with weekends off. I worked for a white family with three small children. The mother was a "madame" and the father was an amateur wrestler. When I took the job, I didn't know what a *madame* was. But I quickly found out after my fourth day on the job. Fortunately, the family home was not where the brothel was. I worked for that family eight weeks. It was not only a unique life experience, it was a nightmare as well.

After standing up to Mama over the issue of my paycheck, she stopped asking that I give her half of my pay. I was then able to save enough money to buy school clothes and supplies for my high school debut. Since my sister didn't work that summer, I used the money I had saved to also take her shopping downtown. We picked out several dresses alike, but in different colors as well as shoes, notebooks, and other supplies we needed. We still could pass for twins, and dressing alike was fun for us. Dee was already in high school, but I was the one who was earning money, and I freely spent it on my sister that summer. The money I earned between my organist and housekeeping jobs that summer was a big help to my parents. However, I paid a very high price for the money I earned while working as a housekeeper.

Several weeks before my summer job ended, one of Mr. Ratliff's friends stopped by, knocked on the front door, and asked to see his friend. When I answered the door, I told him the entire family was out, but he decided he would come in anyway and asked me for something cold to drink. I had seen Marco several times before that particular night but never really paid him any attention because he made me uncomfortable. Since I was referred to as "the colored girl," I stayed out of the way whenever company came by and really didn't think much about why this guy always stared at me whenever he visited. I assumed he wasn't used to seeing coloreds, especially one with green eyes and freckles.

Marco came into the kitchen where I was working. I hurried with my chores to get the dishes washed and kitchen cleaned so I could go home for the weekend. He took several bottles of beer from the Kelvinator, sat at the kitchen table, and made himself comfortable as he drank the beer—all the while staring at me real weird like. He started talking and asking me lots of questions about myself, like how old I was and if I had a boyfriend. Although I was puzzled why he was talking to me like that, I courteously answered him and told him I was sixteen and, no, I didn't have a boyfriend. Little did I know that this predator had set his sights on me as his prey.

I stepped into the pantry to put away the last two pots I'd just washed and dried. The next thing I remember was the pantry door being flung open and Marco grabbing me from behind. He spun me around to face him. Next he backed me up against the wall and started kissing me really hard on the mouth. I pulled my head away and screamed at him to stop, all the while frantically trying to push him off me, but his grip was too strong for me to break. He just ignored my pleas to stop. We struggled in that pantry for what seemed like a long time, but probably only a few seconds had passed. Marco was breathing heavily, and I could smell his beer breath as he muttered obscenities and continued tussling with me. Finally, his strength prevailed over me. He pushed me to the floor, pulled up my dress, ripped off my panties, and forcibly pushed himself inside me. The pain I felt was sharp and burning. I was powerless against him. All I could do was cry. The weight of his body kept me pinned there on that floor until he finished having his way with me. After what seemed like forever, he got up off me and quickly slipped out of the house, leaving me lying on that floor.

When I saw blood and felt pain in my legs, I knew I had been raped—I was no longer an innocent sixteen-year-old. I cried out *Oh! Jesus!* and winced from the pain as I stood to my feet. I fumbled with my clothes to straighten myself up. I stumbled to the bathroom, cleaned up the blood on me, and went home. Nervous and afraid, I was too shaken to tell anyone what has just happened to me. Somehow, I felt like it was my fault. I kept asking myself, *What had I done to cause this to happen to me?* For a long time after that, I carried the burden of that painful event deep inside of me, not even telling my sister or letting the Ratliff's know what their friend had done to me. *They probably wouldn't have taken my word anyway over their white friend, so I said nothing and finished out my last two weeks as their housekeeper.* I never saw Marco again after that. I hated myself. Several months later, I finally told my sister. She didn't know exactly what to say to me, but the look of concern that was in her eyes was comfort enough for me at that time.

High school started the next month, and I quickly threw myself into my books. My tenth-grade year was a blur. The business education course I signed up for consisted of English, typing, shorthand, business math, and science. I did very well in all my classes except science. The shorthand was a big help to me with my English classes and vice versa, especially with prepositional phrases and punctuation. My typing speed was now up to fifty-five words per minute, and I could take shorthand at forty words per minute.

Making As, like my sister easily did, was a hard goal for me to reach. I could only manage to get Bs, Cs, and a few Ds. My focus was merely on getting a passing grade rather than excelling and doing my best work. Being reminded how smart Dee was eventually helped me recognize that I was not a bookworm nor was I as diligent about my schoolwork as she was. However, I was a star pupil in my typing and shorthand classes, and that was good enough for me. Of course, my parents didn't think much of my interest in typing. Dee was encouraged to think about attending college. I was never encouraged by my parents to go on to college. Perhaps it was because I let it be known that I wasn't interested in more school after I graduated, but getting a job and making money was clearly what I wanted to do. I finished my first year of high school with good grades.

My second year of high school started off with a bang. My classes were exciting because I selected the business administration curriculum, and I was determined to do well in all my classes. Although my primary interest was strong for the business world to become a secretary, I was also curious about the possibility of being a radio announcer. Ironically, one of the local black radio broadcasters came to my school for career day, and I quickly pushed my way up to him through all the students in the crowded auditorium and asked a ton of questions about the mixing board (that's what the old radio equipment was called before digital audio automation software was developed).

Mr. Sampson was his name. He was tall, well-spoken, light skinned, and looked to be a cross between an American Indian and an African American. He listened to me talk and patiently answered all my questions. He had piercing eyes as if he was looking right through me. We talked a long time about broadcasting. He asked me if I was serious about learning how to operate radio equipment. When I assured him I was, he said he would gladly teach me how to run a mixing board and gave me his phone number to call him whenever I was ready. Man oh man, was I excited about meeting Mr. Sampson! My imagination began to soar, and I decided right then and there that I would see him again.

I was such a naive sixteen-year-old. *You'd think that after being raped once, I'd be alert to covert overtures from an older man instead of still having a trusting heart—but I wasn't.* If only I could have seen the collision course I was on.

Secretly, I found myself fascinated by this handsome man's interest in me, coupled with some feminine curiosity about him. Finding myself strangely attracted to Mr. Sampson should have scared me, but it didn't nor did I recognize that, once again, I was in the crosshairs of another predator.

On my way home from school after that career day assembly, I found myself thinking about Mr. Sampson a lot. He told me he was thirty-three but certainly didn't look that old, and it didn't bother me that he *was* that old. Maybe it was his beautiful olive-toned skin. Perhaps it was his straight black hair that framed his Native American-looking face that made me think about him so much. Whatever the reason, I secretly decided to call him after the Christmas holidays were over.

8

False Love

False face must hide what the false heart doth know.

—Shakespeare, *Macbeth*

The year 1963 was when I learned what love was *not*. The last six months of my eleventh grade of high school were going to be wonderful, so I thought. Instead, my worst nightmare knocked on the door of my soul.

By the second week in January, anxiety was constantly tugging at me to contact Mr. Sampson about those mixing board lessons. Part of me was still very interested in learning that broadcasting tool, but another part of me was flattered by the attention he had shown me. For a long time after my rape, I felt ugly, but that feeling disappeared when I thought of Mr. Sampson. So while walking home from school, I decided to call him to say I was ready for the mixing board lesson he promised me.

I nervously made the call. At the beginning of our conversation, Mr. Sampson insisted that I call him Henri. He seemed happy that I was still interested in exploring my interest in broadcasting. We agreed to meet the next day, so he gave me his address and directions to his house. The next day was Tuesday, January 15, and just so happened to be my sister's birthday. Letting Henri teach me the mixing board would be my secret. I was afraid if Dee found out about Henri, she would tell on me probably because of his age as well as her concerns that perhaps I wouldn't be safe. It was hard for me to keep secrets from Dee because we told each other everything. We even knew each other's friends. This situation was different. I told myself I'd tell her about my broadcast lessons after I finished them. *But looking back now, not telling my sister about my plan was probably my way of avoiding the very valid warning she would have given me.*

When I got up that Tuesday morning, I wished Dee a happy birthday and proceeded to get dressed just as if I was going to school. As I was dressing, the notion popped into my head to skip school that day and simply hang out with Henri. I had never, ever done anything like that before. I knew I'd get into big trouble if my mother found out what I was planning, so I carefully went through all the normal motions I ordinarily went through to get ready for school so my plan wouldn't be detected. I caught the trolley but did not get off at my regular stop. Four more stops put me at Henri's street. I got off the trolley and began walking to his house. It was very cold that day, but I was dressed warmly. I was very nervous and a little scared someone would see me and tell my mother I wasn't in school that day. That turned out to be the least of my worries.

I found Henri's house and rang the bell. He opened the door and gave me a big smile and told me how glad he was to see me. After taking off my coat, he asked me if I wanted to join him for breakfast because he was getting ready to prepare his. I agreed, and we ate breakfast together. After finishing my meal, I subtly glanced around the place for the broadcasting equipment I went there to learn about. I saw tons of record albums stacked in piles around the living room along the baseboards, but no big equipment that looked like a mixing board. In addition to being a radio announcer, Henri also worked as a disc jockey, and the record albums were part of his private collection.

We talked for what seemed like hours, and I felt very comfortable in Henri's company. He was quick-witted and funny. I laughed at all his jokes. Next he asked me if I would help him sort some albums for an upcoming sock hop he had to Dee-jay. The task took us almost two hours to finish because he had a lot of albums. When I looked at the clock, it was lunchtime, and I was hungry again; so Henri fixed me a huge bologna sandwich and poured me a tall glass of cold sweet milk. When I finished eating and got up from the table to put my empty glass in the sink, Henri came up behind me, hugged me, and cunningly convinced me to take a nap with him. He said his head was aching, and he needed to lie down for a short while. It was dumb of me to fall for that line. Somehow, I was still a trusting and naïve soul, so I shyly agreed. There was something very intoxicating about Henri that compelled me to follow his lead, and I felt powerless to stop myself.

As I slowly lay beside him on his small bed, a little voice inside of me whispered that I had better get out of there. As I raised myself up off the mattress to crawl out of his bed to leave, I felt Henri's hand on my back pull me closer to him on the bed. I noticed he had taken off his pants. He rolled over on top of me and kept saying real softly, "Don't fight me. I must have you." Then he wouldn't stop kissing me as he lifted up my skirt, slid my underwear to one side of my leg, and, very gently, entered me. I didn't feel the sharp pain and burning that I felt when Marco pushed himself inside of me. Henri panted really hard for a few seconds and finally stopped pushing his body against mine as he rolled off me. He looked exhausted and was real still as he quietly lay beside me on the other side of that small bed. How could I have not seen this coming? *Somehow, I knew there wouldn't be a lesson on the mixing board. What was I thinking to trust this man?* It took me about twenty minutes to clean myself up and gather my things to leave. Henri crawled off his bed and put his pants back on. Feeling ashamed and embarrassed didn't begin to describe how I felt inside. I started berating myself. I was an idiot to have put myself in that position. This time, I was completely to blame for what had just happened to me!

As I was putting my coat on and went to the front door to leave, Henri leaned over, kissed me on my cheek, and gave me money to catch a cab home. Next he put on a jacket and walked me outside to wait with me. While we were standing on the corner waiting on a taxi, Henri seemed very different to me. I wasn't quite sure how different, but it was a *good* different. His glance was soft and tender as he told me how much he enjoyed his day with me and insisted that we get together again. A cab drove up; I said goodbye and climbed into the cab. That chilly January day became more of a blur to me as I rehearsed in my head what I should have done instead of what actually happened to me at Henri's house. For reasons I didn't understand, I wasn't upset with him for forcing himself on me since I wasn't hurt. Perhaps I wanted it to happen.

Arriving home twenty minutes later than usual from school didn't concern Mom too much. But Dee looked at me funny and immediately knew something was different with me. When we were alone in our room, she kept asking me what happened to me that day, and I continued telling her *nothing*. Finally, I couldn't keep my secret any longer; and before we fell off to sleep that night, I told Dee the whole story. Her eyes got wide, and her jaw dropped in shock. But she was the perfect sister and friend, as she always is, when she said, "I'm glad that you're okay, and he didn't hurt you."

She then asked me if he used protection. I asked her, "What's that?"

As she looked at me in amazement, she said, "I sure hope you didn't get pregnant. You know what Mama said she'd do to us if that happens?" Getting pregnant never occurred to me. After that conversation with my sister, I wasn't sure whether I would see Henri again.

To take my mind off Henri, I concentrated on my schoolwork so I could earn good grades over the remaining two semesters left in my eleventh grade. Several weeks went by, and I had not called him, but Henri called me several times. He wanted to know when he could see me again, and I told him I couldn't see him again because my parents would not approve of me dating a man his age. I was sixteen, and he was thirty-three. Henri told me I was very mature, and he was quite surprised to learn that I was only sixteen years old. He went on to say that after I spent that day with him the month before, I was now a significant part of his life, and he wouldn't let me run away from him that easily. I agreed to see him again just as soon as I could sneak away. Strangely, I never got around to visiting Henri again because my life took an unexpected turn.

When Valentine's Day arrive four weeks later, I realized I had not had my period. It was Dee who noticed that I was sleeping more than usual and eating more food than I ordinarily did. She was very knowledgeable about the "facts of life" and figured it out that I was pregnant. I was shocked at that possibility! This definitely was a big *Oh! Jesus* moment for me! *Before Dee mentioned this, I really hadn't paid much attention to the fact that I had been feeling tired and nauseated.* I found myself wondering, *How could I have gotten pregnant this time?* The mystery was overwhelming to me since I didn't get pregnant when Marco raped me the summer before.

Dee and I waited until Mom and Dad went to bed before we talked about my situation. When Dee asked me what I was going to do, I quickly told her that I was keeping my baby and that I needed to tell Henri I was expecting his child. When Dee and I first started our periods, our mother did her best to put the fear of God in us about ever getting pregnant. Although we believed our parents loved us, Mom's warnings about what she'd do to us if we *screwed around* (as she put it) and got pregnant didn't sound like love to me. Mom went so far as to threaten to throw us out on the street if either of us ever came home in a family way. I guess deep down inside, I didn't think our mother would do something as cold and heartless as throwing us out if we got pregnant.

By my calculations, I was certain I was four weeks along since I knew exactly the day I conceived, January 15—the day I skipped school. Finally, I called Henri and told him that I was pregnant. He was very happy about me being in a family way; but I decided to wait a little while longer before I told my mother about the baby. I went about my normal routine and stayed out of Mom's way so she wouldn't notice that I was gaining weight.

School was out in April for Easter break, and I slept late every morning. However, my entire world came crashing down around me very early on a Thursday morning. My mother suddenly opened the door to my room, pulled the covers off me, and said, "Vee, the Holy Spirit told me you're pregnant!" Shock and amazement paralyzed me. I slowly sat up in my bed, not really knowing what to say, so I hung my head in condemnation. Mama continued fussing and saying ugly things to me until I burst into tears and confessed it was true and that I was three months along.

She said some more ungodly things to me and called me a little whore. She asked me who the father was, and I told her Henri. She continually threatened to throw me out on the street. I cried and pleaded with her not to do that.

Mom left our room, came right back again, and continued fussing some more. She angrily shouted at me, "Vee, you are not having this bastard child! How dare you disgrace me like this! I will not stand for the neighbors to know what you have done! Your Dad will take care of this!" She would not listen when I told her I wanted to keep my baby. She became even more enraged when I told her that Henri wanted to marry me. It was very difficult for me to think clearly enough to figure things out for myself especially since I didn't know what my choices were as a pregnant sixteen-year-old.

When Mom finally stopped her ranting, I took a moment to collect my thoughts. I was confused and full of questions. How could Jesus tell her my secret? What did she mean that my Dad would take care of this? For Mom to be the churchgoing Christian that she portrayed herself as, why did she put more value on her reputation and what people thought of her than on the life that I had inside of me?

She couldn't have loved me to say those horrible things and to threaten to murder my child. Fear of what would happen to me was so mentally crippling until I could not even pray. Somehow I thought my friend, Jesus, was also angry with me for getting pregnant.

9

My Greatest Loss

A lost thing could I never find,
Nor a broken thing mend.

—Hilaire Belloc (1870-1953)

A Dad is supposed to protect his child. This time, mine did not. After the bombshell dropped that I was pregnant, my mother punished me. And because school was still in session, I had to come straight home from school and go to my room. I was also not allowed to use the phone and was told not to ever speak to Henri again.

I was very upset over the horrible things my mother had said to me, and the threats she expressed. The night Mom told Dad the whole story, I didn't leave my room for dinner because I didn't want to face him when she told him about my pregnancy.

I did, however, sneak out of my room to quietly hide behind the kitchen door in clear earshot of their conversation so I could listen to everything that was being said about me. Dad continued eating his dinner while Mom went on and on about how I had disgraced the family by getting pregnant. Still Dad said nothing.

Next I heard my mother tell him she knew of a doctor who lived in Washington DC that did abortions and could take care of *this* problem. She said she would not allow my bastard child to be born and give her reputation a black eye! Her tone of voice was full of rage, and every angry word that came out of her mouth cut me to the core. Finally, she demanded that Dad find that doctor and get me *fixed* immediately.

While still standing behind the door, I peeked through the crack of the door and saw my Dad holding his head in his hands. He was visibly bothered by what he was hearing. *Dad only held his head in his hand when he was at a loss for words or bewildered.* His silence sickened me. Sad feelings welled up inside of me, and I began to cry quietly. I felt abandoned by my Dad for not coming to my defense again, disagreeing with my mother's plan and adamantly telling her that abortion was not the best solution. Instead, he simply agreed to her demands to locate the doctor. Listening to my mother badger Dad with her self-righteous babble nauseated me; and I quietly moved away from the door I was hiding behind, went to my room, and cried myself to sleep.

During the next two weeks, I was a mess. I couldn't concentrate on my schoolwork, and I did not talk to my parents when I was home. My life was in turmoil. I was three and a half months pregnant—the fourteenth week to be exact—scared and clueless about what was about to happen to me. I thought the fluttering I felt in my belly was gas and anxiety. I found out later that what I felt inside was not gas, but my baby moving. Feeling abandoned by the two people I thought really loved me caused so much anxiety deep inside until I was convinced there was no one I could go to for help. Calling Henri was out of the question. Part of me didn't want him to know my parents were capable of forcing me to have the abortion, and another part of me was afraid he would also turn his back on me despite his assurances that he wanted to marry me.

My whole world crumbled on Tuesday, April 23rd. Mom made me stay home from school that day and told me that a doctor was coming to our house to *take care of my problem*. She told me to take a very hot bath, put on my nightgown, and wait in the back bedroom of our house until she told me otherwise. The back bedroom was Dad's room. After she told me about the doctor coming to the house, I knew that day would be a bad one for me. My mind began to race. I thought of running away, but where would I go? Who would help me? Feeling defeated and alone, I resigned myself to the brutal truth that my parents were actually going through with their plans of killing my baby. I thought I could also die during the process. Although I prayed and called out to my best friend, Jesus, I didn't feel his presence and felt my prayers were useless. I believed Jesus was also angry with me.

I took a bath as I was told to do and went into my Mom's room to get dressed. Her bedroom was in the front of our house. As I put on my nightgown, I looked out of the window and saw a tall slim older man get out of his car and stagger across the street as he walked toward our front door carrying a black doctor's bag. If this person was the doctor, he looked as if he was drunk. I was terrified to realize that my life would be in the hands of that drunken individual. Dazed, weeping, and full of despair, I stumbled back to Dad's room and sat down on the bed to wait for my nightmare to begin.

Moments later, the back bedroom door opened; and there stood my mother holding some rope and the man with the black bag whom she introduced as the doctor. She told me to lie down on the bed so the doctor could take care of me. As I reluctantly lay back on the bed, the voices of the doctor and my mother became muffled. I truly believed I would die that day. My mother used clothesline to securely tie each of my arms to the two top bedposts, and loosely tied each leg to the two bottom bedposts. *I figured Mom tied me to the bed to keep me from running.*

The doctor fumbled in his black bag and pulled out a long instrument that looked like a knitting needle. Next he dipped the tip of the instrument in alcohol. When he stepped closer to me, I definitely smelled alcohol on his breath. I found myself thinking that he must have needed a few drinks to numb his senses for the murder he was about to commit. Then terror struck me at the possibility that this drunken doctor could permanently damage me if that object slipped while inside of me, causing me not to ever bear another child.

I closed my eyes tight as he raised my legs up, inserted a cold speculum inside me, turned the screw that cranked it open, inserted that long needlelike tool inside, and punctured my uterus with it. The pain I felt was like a bee sting on the inside. Then the doctor reached in his black bag again and pulled out a large package of gauze. He wrapped the gauze around the top of the instrument until it looked like a small ball on the end. Next he put the gauze ball into the bowl of saline solution he had prepared and pushed the gauze pack through the speculum deep inside of me. Finally, he lowered my legs and pulled the covers over me.

Through the blurred words, I heard the doctor say to me that my abdomen would soon begin hurting in about two hours—that would be labor—and in several more hours, I would "pass" the baby before the end of the day. As he gathered his supplies and put them back in his black bag, he turned to my mother and told her that I would be okay by the next day and that I should rest. Then he opened the bedroom door and let himself out.

By now, I was sobbing uncontrollably while my mother untied the clothesline that had bound me to the four-poster bed. After my arms and legs were freed, I could move again. While lying in Daddy's bed motionless and in shock, I looked up at my mother and asked, "Why, Momma?" She never answered me. Instead, she placed a slop bucket at the end of the bed for me to use when the baby came out, locked the door, and left me all alone to suffer through the gut-wrenching pains of giving birth to a dead baby. Within two hours, I started having excruciating pain in my stomach, and I began to bleed.

As the day turned into night, I tossed and turned from one side of the bed to the other, hurting so badly that I wished for death. Floating in and out of sane moments, I remember praying and asking God to have mercy on me. I felt so worthless and dirty. But something inside of me tugged at my spirit to not give up. As I writhed in pain the entire day, indescribable feelings of subtle anger toward my parents started to mount inside me. I just couldn't comprehend how, according to them, getting rid of my baby was the best thing. Finally, after being locked in Dad's room for what seemed like an eternity, I felt pain and pressure in my bottom that felt like I would have a bowel movement at any moment. So I got up, staggered to the bucket, and sat on it. A warm lump slid out of me. I stood up and looked into the bucket to see what my body had just expelled. I saw a tiny, tiny fully formed baby. It was a boy. I whispered my child's name, Ronnie, and started crying again and whispered, "*Oh, Jesus*, where are you?" I pulled myself together and, once again, looked at the glob of lifeless matter in the bucket and asked my baby's forgiveness for what had just happened.

Around 9:30 PM that night, my mother finally unlocked the bedroom door and came into the room. Her concerns were not for me, but simply to see if I had passed the baby and to tell me Dad was ready to go to bed and wanted me out of his room. When Mom looked into the bucket, she knew everything was over. I raised myself up slowly off Dad's bed and walked past my mother out of that back bedroom to the bathroom. After cleaning myself up, I went to my room that I shared with my sister, crawled into my bed, and tried to forget what had just happened to me. Dee was asleep. We never talked about that night. Everyone pretended like it didn't happen.

I never saw what my mother did with my child in the bucket, and I never asked. But after I left out of the bathroom, I remember hearing the toilet flush and Mom rinsing out the bucket in the tub. I assumed she flushed my baby down the toilet. I felt like my heart had just been ripped out of my body. There were a multitude of questions racing around in my brain. How would I tell Henri that I no longer was carrying his child? How do I regain respect for my Dad for not saving me from Mom's wrath? How could my mother claim to be a Christian and coldheartedly watch a doctor strip life from my young body? What was I going to do now?

Although I didn't feel like I was ready to face the world, I went back to school two days later. The bleeding was still heavy, but I just couldn't stay home another day with my mother after what she had done to me. She behaved as if we were one big happy family. I constantly thought to myself, *Could I ever forgive my parents for killing my son?*

Several days later, Henri called to see how I was doing and to tell me he wanted to talk with me about us. He said he also wanted to speak with my parents about our situation, and he didn't want to wait any longer. He went on to say that he was happy about the baby and didn't care about our age difference but wanted to do the right thing and marry me so he could take care of our child and me. After he said all that, I quietly cried on the other end of the phone without him knowing. I thought to myself, *If I had just heard him say those things a week ago, I would have had a refuge to escape my mother's wrath and would still have my son inside me. Perhaps he really did care about me.*

I tried to convince Henri to wait a while longer before speaking to my parents because I was afraid. I needed more time before I broke the news to him that I wasn't pregnant anymore. Henri was insistent on speaking with my parents *that day*, so I agreed for him to come to my house. I paced the floor as I waited for Henri to arrive. I was clueless as to what I would say to him. I never told Mom that he was on his way. When the doorbell rang, I opened the door and sheepishly looked at him and feigned a smile. Henri quickly stole a kiss and started telling me how much he had missed me and reminded me we hadn't spent time together in over three months. I interrupted his ramblings and told him to have a seat while I went to get my mother.

When my mother entered the living room, Henri stood up to greet her. They both sat down. He looked at me, smiled warmly, then began to speak. He told my mother that he was the father of my child, and he wanted to do the right thing by me and marry me. He went on to say that he had a good job and could more than adequately provide for a family.

All the while Henri was talking, Mom sat gracefully in her seat, waiting for him to finish speaking. I never said anything but kept my head down.

Next he asked Mom if she would sign for me to marry him since I wasn't eighteen yet. Then the climate in the room morphed into raging ugliness. Mom shifted her position in her chair and very sternly announced to Henri that she would not sign for me to marry him because I was no longer pregnant, so there would be no wedding. I kept my head down so as not to show my shock to what she said next. Straight-faced, my mother looked Henri in the eye and told him I had had a miscarriage while pushing our heavy washing machine across the floor while doing the laundry two weeks prior.

Henri stood to his feet and looked at me with great pain on his face. Next he turned to my mother and angrily told her she was lying and that he didn't believe a word she was saying to be true. I wouldn't look up at Henri because I didn't want him to think I was agreeable with the lie my mother was telling him. With my head still down, I began to cry.

Then Mom stood to her feet, put her hands on her hips, and told Henri to get out of her house. She added that if he knew what was good for him, he better not ever darken her doorstep again and that he also better leave me alone, or she would make him sorry he ever met me. *It was obvious to me that Henri was no match for my mother!* I think her threat of calling the police was what stopped him from really giving Mom a piece of his mind.

At that point, Henri quickly went to the front door to let himself out, slamming our front door behind him. Mom opened the door and watched him walk away. As he went down our front steps, he turned around and shouted an obscenity back at my mother and told her she would burn in hell for killing his child. Stunned from the bitter exchange between Henri and my mother, I was still glued to my seat when Mom locked the front door behind Henri.

I never saw or heard from Henri again after that day.

10

Back in the Race

> *When green buds hang in the elm like dust*
> *and sprinkle the lime like rain,*
> *forth I wander, forth I must,*
> *and drink of life again.*
>
> —A. E. Housman (1859-1936)

Forgetting April 23 took every ounce of emotional strength I had, and I was determined to press on despite the soul-shaking pain that was still inside of me. I resumed my studies at school and completed the eleventh grade with honors. Dee's graduation that June gave my family a great event to smile about and be happy. And as expected, Dee's final report card was outstanding since she had excelled in all her classes. Our parents behaved like they were pillars of the community, and everything was peachy keen.

Comforting myself with the thought that I would be eighteen in another year and could move away from home helped me get through the day-to-day disdain I felt toward my parents for murdering my son. Where I would go was quite another matter, but at least I knew the first step of that journey was to come up with a plan. Since school was over and summer was fast approaching, I needed to find a job, so I began combing the want ads in the local newspaper. At that point, I was a pretty good typist, so I started looking for any job that advertised a need for a clerk typist. As a backup plan, I placed a job wanted ad in the local newspaper so perspective employers could contact me. My sister also wanted a summer job to earn a little money before going off to college in the fall.

I received several calls from the newspaper ad I placed. One, in particular, was from a woman who said her company needed a junior typist. The duties she described to me certainly sounded like something I could handle. After we exchanged a few pleasantries, she asked me if I could come in the next day for an interview. I immediately said yes!

The training I received in home economics class taught me four basics on how to present myself well in an interview: (1) give a proper handshake, (2) maintain eye contact during the interview, (3) sit straight with good posture, and (4) smile. More than that, I give my Mom credit for instilling in me three absolutes that have influenced my entire life. Mom said, "Vee, as a Negro, you will have to be twice as good as your counterpart when you go to get a job." Mom went on to say, "The first thing they will notice is the color of your skin, so keep it clean and smooth. The second thing they will notice is how you are dressed. So always be neat, clean, and balanced. And the third thing they will notice is how you speak, so talk clearly, and don't chew up your words!"

I was on a serious mission to get that job, and I did! It was a mom-and-pop frozen food distribution company that did home deliveries of bulk food orders. During my interview, the owners were so impressed with me they asked me to start immediately and gave me a quarter above minimum wage as my starting salary. I was very excited about earning $60 a week! That was my very first *real* job. At the end of the interview, I thanked the owners for the opportunity to be their new assistant and floated out of their office!

When I got home, I only shared my excitement with my sister. Although I did tell my mother that I had found a job, I mentioned it in such a matter-of-fact manner that she didn't even respond. It was no surprise to my mother that I accomplished what I set out to do. Since I still had not forgiven them, my relationship with my parents was very strained, and conversations between us were nonexistent.

Next a wonderful thing happened. Another call came in from the ad I had placed. That caller identified himself as an ear, nose, and throat doctor who desperately needed a secretary for his small office. He went on to say he basically needed someone to answer phones, set up patient appointments, and do very light typing. I thought to myself, *This would be perfect for Dee!* So I asked him to hold the line and handed her the phone. She went for the interview, got the job, and was a happy camper! Now we both had ourselves summer jobs and our own money. Life was good.

Working for the frozen food company the summer of '63 was a healing experience for me. I loved the daily hustle and bustle that went on in that busy office—taking phone orders from customers, typing delivery tickets, and, sometimes, even packing frozen food orders—and feeling needed quickly helped me feel good about myself for the contribution I was making to my job.

One day while helping out in the warehouse, fate dealt me a surprise left hook. One of the packers kept teasing me about being so serious and rarely smiling. His name was Shoff. He was funny, and I easily laughed at the funny things he said. Since Henri, I had not given myself permission to become interested in boys again. But this guy would not leave me alone. After realizing that Shoff really liked me, I started smiling back at him. Before long, we were eating our lunches together. The attraction I felt for Shoff was exhilarating, and it definitely was mutual. He was tall, athletic, soft-spoken, very handsome, and had a unique twinkle in his eyes. I turned seventeen that summer; he was eighteen and also in his last year of school like me, except he attended school in North Carolina. The coolest thing about Shoff was his dancing skill!

Sometimes, he would play his radio real loud while packing customer orders. I could see him through the breezeway window dancing in and out of the freezer as he pulled those orders. The radio was loud enough for everyone to hear it in the business office. Several times, he would come into the front office, pull me up out of my chair, and dance with me. Shoff was a happy fella, and I found myself soaking up every bit of the attention he showered upon me. By the time our summer jobs were over, Shoff and I were going steady. We promised to be each other's prom date. That meant I would go to North Carolina to his prom, and he would come back to Maryland for mine. For the first time in a very long while, I felt special.

That September, I began my last year in high school. My typing had really improved from the job experience I gained working during the summer. My typing speed had increased by ten words a minute. My goal was to accurately type sixty-five words a minute by the time I graduated, and I was well on my way of accomplishing that goal.

I carried on with my normal school routines and duties as church musician and also wrote Shoff one letter a week. We saw each other during the Thanksgiving and Christmas breaks and were glad that school would soon be over for both of us. On January 1, I started to count the days until I turned eighteen. I had some pretty definite plans in my head for when that time in my life arrived.

In early March of 1964, my church held its senior choir anniversary. As part of that celebration, visiting singing groups came to my church and performed in a Gospel songfest. I was the designated church musician for that service because Mr. Brown was given the night off. One group in particular caught my eye. It was a six-member family group of five brothers and one sister, locally known as the Open Heart Singers. Three of the brothers played guitars including the lead singer, whom I especially noticed. At the end of the service, that handsome guy I had noticed earlier came up to me at the piano and introduced himself. He had the nicest smile, perfect white teeth, and mesmerizing hazel eyes. His name was Sack. We talked for a while, and then he asked me if he could call me sometime. I felt it would be rude to brush him off since my church had just hosted his family group, so I gave him my number although I had a boyfriend.

My senior year passed very quickly, and prom time rolled around in May. Because I had become very independent, my decision to catch a train to North Carolina to attend my boyfriend's prom was not an issue for my parents or me. They generally left me alone, and I basically stayed out of their way. Shoff proudly escorted me to his prom and introduced me to all his friends. After being spun around on the dance floor for four hours, my feet were hurting badly. But not once did I say no when he wanted to dance. I was determined to keep up with Shoff and all his fancy footwork. After his graduation ceremony the next day, I caught a late train back to Baltimore, exhausted but happy.

The following week was my prom. Shoff came up from Carolina and escorted me there. This time, he really cut up on the dance floor, and I had one heck of a time keeping up with him. No doubt, all the back flips, splits, and jitterbugging he did all night tired him out more than he wanted me to know. But he loved all the attention he received for his dancing prowess. There were lots of after parties and early breakfast get-togethers that I so looked forward to attending with him but never made it. Instead, I ended up sitting in his mom's basement angry while Shoff slept on the floor because he was really tired. Needless to say, my senior prom was a big disappointment.

By the time summer was in full bloom, I was focused on finding a secure job and decided that should be with the government. I filled out an application for a clerk-typist position with the Department of Defense. I prayed and asked my friend Jesus to help me get that job, and I ended my prayer with my usual, "Thank you, Lord!" Somehow, I knew in my heart of hearts that I'd hear back from Uncle Sam and get that job. I also knew the hiring process would be lengthy since background and reference checks had to be done to make sure I was a fit candidate to fill the position, but I wasn't worried one bit. You could say my faith was rock solid. In the meantime, however, I needed to start earning money to buy myself a new car; so I took a position in the emergency department at a local hospital as a clerk typist.

In August, Shoff asked me to marry him and I immediately accepted. He was nineteen; I was eighteen. I was so determined to get away from my home life with my mother that getting married seemed like the perfect out. We set the wedding date for October 3, 1964—one day after Shoff's birthday. I bought my wedding gown, ordered invitations, and started the ball rolling for my exodus adventure. I had turned eighteen the month before and was excited about the possibility of moving away from home.

Admittedly, I overlooked some bad stuff during our courtship, like how much of a flirt Shoff was and his insatiable sexual appetite that I had difficulty keeping up with. Going ahead with this marriage was an obvious compromise for me, but I didn't care. Getting married was the best way, so I thought, to move away from home without flack from my mother and father. But when my phone rang two weeks before I was to mail out the wedding invitations, I could no longer look the other way about Shoff's behavior. You could say the grits had hit the proverbial fan. The caller was a friend from church. Her name was Lila. Lila told me that I wouldn't like what she had to tell me, but felt I needed to know about my fiancé's behavior before I went through with a wedding I'd later regret. From the sound of her voice, I knew what I would hear was serious.

Lila told me that Shoff had invited her to accompany him to the mall, under the pretense of helping him find a gift for me. She agreed and met him at his apartment. After all, we were friends and had all previously hung out together. Before she could take a seat and wait for him to put his coat on, he lured her into his bedroom to show her a picture of us. Never believing that she was in any danger, she took him at his word and stepped in his room to see the picture. He immediately grabbed her, threw her down on his bed, and tried to force himself on her. Because Lila was a heavyset girl, she was able to beat him off her and fight her way out of his room to escape. After verifying Lila's story, I canceled the wedding. Of course, Shoff tried to convince me that Lila was lying. Fortunately, I wasn't that desperate to leave home to marry that rascal, so I held on to my self-respect and didn't give in to his pleas for us to still get married.

Although I was disappointed about not getting married, I knew it was a bad idea to marry a man that had a fidelity issue. So I hung up my wedding dress on the back of my bedroom door until another marriage opportunity presented itself.

Ironically, a week after breaking my engagement to Shoff, I received a phone call from Sack, the handsome fella I had met six months earlier. He told me he had misplaced my number but found it in the pocket of the suit he had worn the night he sang at my church. He went on to say he had been drafted, was now in the army, and was stationed locally. He added that he had thought about me a lot since we met. Then he asked if he could take me out on a date, and I quickly accepted his invitation. *The way I figured, he would be a good distraction for me to forget about my broken engagement.*

Some people believe that good things come in threes, and I was inclined to believe that adage after the next two things happened to me that September. Three days after hearing from Sack, the call I had been expecting from the government came. I was told I had gotten the job I applied for, and my start date would be December 7. Two days after that, the car dealer where I had placed a credit application to buy a car called to say my application had been approved, and I could come in and pick up my brand-new Chevy Impala. I felt like I was on top of the world!

Sack and I started dating in September 1964. I had recently had my eighteenth birthday. He was very courteous and respectable. Early into the courtship, he asked me what my favorite flower was. Although he was always late coming to pick me up, he never failed to have a box of candy or flowers in his hands each time he came to see me. When he found out I loved gladiolas, he regularly showered me with colorful bouquets of them. My mother loved him! Little did she know that his regular Thursday-night visits to pick me up involved a weekly tryst at a local motel.

Christmas of that year, Sack and I became engaged. Although we had only dated for about three months, I agreed to marry him. I had a dream that Sack would receive Orders to go overseas. Sure enough, four months later the Orders came. He was scheduled to go overseas to Vietnam. The war was going on and he wasn't sure when he would be home again but didn't expect to be gone longer than twelve months. As luck would have it, I was "late" and thought that I was pregnant again. This time, I wasn't taking any chances with my mother reacting to this pregnancy the way she reacted to my first one. Since I still lived in her house, her rules prevailed, but I vowed she would never kill another child of mine. So if my getting pregnant could blemish her reputation, she would have to deal with it because I was not having another abortion for no one! Once I told Sack my period was late, he insisted that we get married before he left for the war. We set the wedding date for May 8, 1965. Since I was expecting to leave the state of Maryland after getting married, I resigned my job as church organist.

There wasn't enough time to send out fancy invitations, so I sent telegrams to some family members and a select group of friends. Exactly one day before the wedding, Sack told me he was about to be a Daddy. The girl he dated before me was nine months pregnant and due to have their child at anytime. I grew numb inside when he dropped that bomb on me. I had to think quickly—should I forgive him for telling me this news a day before our wedding and go ahead with marrying him or walk away? I felt it would be best that I go ahead with my plans and marry Sack anyway. Clearly, our relationship did not have a solid foundation from the get-go, and I ignored all the signals around me not to go through with the marriage.

I forged ahead anyway and put together a very simple wedding ceremony and reception at my church. The wedding was quite nice despite the fact that Sack was an hour late arriving at the church. Dad walked me down the aisle and gave me away. As a former chef, he also did the cooking for the reception. My mother did not come to my wedding, never told me why; and I never asked.

I looked forward to packing my few belongings and finally moving away from my parents' home! For my honeymoon, as it were, I spent the first nineteen days of my marriage at an army base in Virginia with my husband before he shipped out to Vietnam. The day Sack boarded the bus en route overseas, I cried my little heart out when I found out I could not go with him but had to move back home with my parents until he returned from Vietnam—only the soldiers were allowed to be in a war zone. My exodus plan had failed miserably! As I gathered myself and dried my tears as the bus pulled off, a soldier approached me and introduced himself. He said he noticed me in the crowd of other women who were saying goodbye to their husbands who were also shipping out to Vietnam. He asked me my name and gave me his card to contact him if I needed anything.

Although I was distraught that day, I was quite impressed with the concern and genuine compassion Sergeant Bennett showed me as the wife of a fellow soldier. I remember thinking to myself how nice it was for that gentleman to be concerned about me. After packing my things, I straightened up the room we had lived in for nineteen days and sadly drove myself back to Baltimore and patiently waited on my husband's first letter.

Two weeks later, I received a letter from Sergeant Bennett. As I looked at the letter before opening it up, I thought it somewhat strange for that soldier to be writing me. However, when I read his letter, I completely understood his motives for approaching me when I was crying outside of that army bus. The sergeant's letter actually propositioned me to allow him to *comfort me* while my husband was away and blatantly solicited my intimate companionship. I might have been young and somewhat naïve, but I knew the sergeant had crossed the line.

I was incensed at the nerve of that man and immediately wrote Sack and enclosed the sergeant's letter. Turns out, the sergeant broke an ethics rule by propositioning another soldier's wife and was punished; he lost his stripes and was demoted to a private.

11

All That Glitters Ain't Gold

Not all that tempts your wand'ring eyes
And heedless hearts, is lawful prize;
Nor all, that glisters, gold.

—Thomas Gray (1716-1771)

I was a new bride, just eighteen years old, and my life had taken a U-turn on the road I so desperately tried to get off. Going back home was not in the plan once I got married. So I had to suck up my pride and move back to my parents' home on the condition that I'd only stay with them for a few months or until my husband came home from Vietnam, whichever was the shortest time frame. I offered to pay rent while I stayed with my parents, but they refused to accept any money from me. I wondered to myself, *What alien had taken over my mother's body? She always loved money for as long as I knew her. What was different now?* I said thank you and carried on.

Being back at my parents' home was an easier adjustment than I thought it would be. My mother was kinder to me, but the tension between us was still there, and I believed she knew in her heart there was unfinished business between us. But I kept a respectful attitude toward her and went about my daily routine as if everything was simply grand. Dad, on the other hand, always tried making conversation with me whenever we were both in the same room together. Although no words were ever spoken between us about the Henri situation and my first pregnancy, I knew a black cloud still hung heavy over Dad's head about that. In my eyes, he was a much sadder man now; perhaps he regularly wrestled with demons of *regret* for not intervening in my behalf when my mother told him to find that doctor, and for his role two years earlier in murdering his first grandchild.

After about a week, I finally settled into a new routine at my parents' home of going to work and coming home. At first, it felt really strange coming in from work and not preparing dinner like I did before I got married. But I quickly found other enjoyable things to do with my free time in the evenings, like visiting friends or going to the movies.

Two weeks after my husband left for Vietnam, much to my surprise, my period came. For a split second, I regretted the decision to marry him before he left for Vietnam; man oh man, how I wished I had just waited. It had been four weeks late, so naturally, I thought I was pregnant. It became apparent to me that my already-late cycle was compounded by two circumstances: (1) the stress of putting together my abstract shotgun marriage and (2) my soon-to-be husband telling me a day before my wedding that he had a baby on the way.

(Let me back up and give you some details on why my husband did not trust me. When Dee and I were growing up, my mother regularly took in foster children into our home whose parents were unable to care for them. Two adolescent sisters—Mabel and Catherine—came to live with us when they were 9 and 10. They stayed with us 6 years until they blossomed into voluptuous teenagers. Then Mom sent them away after she suspected Dad of showing a little too much interest in them. The next foster child that Mom took in was a 10-day old baby girl by the name of Earlene. She stayed in our home until she was also a teenager. Mom sent her away because she became unmanageable. The last foster child that Mom took in was a 3-year old little angel by the name of Marian. She only stayed with Mom and Dad for about 6 months. One week after Marian came to our home; Sack met her once while we were dating.)

When I wrote and told my husband that we weren't having a baby, he wrote a nasty letter back, accusing me of tricking him into marrying me. He even accused me of not telling him that little Marian was my child, but said it was okay if she was, since he didn't tell me about his soon-to-be-born baby until the day before our wedding. Sack actually thought Marian was my child because she resembled me, but never expressed that thought until he put it in that letter.

When I read his letter of outrage, I was somewhat shocked by his reaction especially since it was he who insisted we get married before he went overseas to ensure I would be around when he got back from the war! Clearly, the root of his anger was his distrust of me given the fact that (1) I was not pregnant when we got married and (2) he believed little Marian—my mother's 3-year old foster child—was mine and that I had not told him about her. I began doubting the strength of our union and was convinced my marriage was doomed to fail.

My long workdays helped the weeks and months pass quickly. Despite the cloud of distrust that was over my head, I still wrote Sack one letter a day and two on Sunday. I believed a steady flow of letters from home would help him cope with the hazards he had to face during the war and minimize our marital stress. I also sent him occasional care packages chock-full of goodies.

After we got through the issues of me not being pregnant and little Marian not being my daughter, another crisis arose. Three months after the wedding, I began receiving a $27 government check. What I wasn't aware of was that Sack had established two allotment disbursements: one to his mother as the primary recipient, and another to me as the secondary recipient. Seven months into our marriage, Uncle Sam caught the error that I was the wife and reversed the allotment allocations. In December, I started receiving a check for $105.

I wrote my husband thanking him for the extra money I had received. Once again, he wrote me a scathing letter, and I didn't understand why. He accused me of stealing his mother's money. My explanation that I had nothing to do with the change to the allotment distribution fell on deaf ears. Sack seriously believed I orchestrated the situation of changing his allocations. He called me a terrible and low person for "taking pennies from his mother." This was yet another serious fight while he was away.

After Uncle Sam notified Sack that they had readjusted his allotment allocation, he apologized to me for the mean things he accused me of. However, after that last blowup with all the hurtful words he wrote, the content and volume of my letters immediately and measurably changed. I guess I was struggling again with forgiveness. However, if there was any doubt in my mind about the survivability of my marriage, my answer to that question came in the letter I received from my husband one month before he was due to come home—in time for our one-year anniversary, so I thought!

A nicely wrapped present accompanied Sack's letter. The package contained a beautiful set of diamond rings. His letter stated those rings replaced the small diamond rings he hastily gave me when we were married. Next his letter said two very disturbing things: (1) he was re-upping so his mother could have free medical insurance, and (2) he wouldn't be home for another six months! I wrote him back and suggested that I could add his mom to my employment insurance plan. That way, she could have excellent health care coverage, and he wouldn't have to re-up. But his next letter clearly said no to my suggestion. He wouldn't allow me to add my mother-in-law to my insurance coverage. *Things were very different then in the insurance industry; adding my mother-in-law to my health insurance was an allowable transaction.*

After I finished reading his bombshell letter, I thought to myself, *Here we go again!* Indescribable anger welled up inside of me. The unilateral decision Sack had made without conferring with me drove the last proverbial nail in our marriage coffin. At no point in his letter was there any inferred consideration of me as his spouse to discuss the decision to re-up for another six months. It was obvious I was not thought of as a wife, but more like a young child bride. In my outrage I clearly remember thinking, *So you're re-upping, huh? Well, re-up this! The marriage is over!*

I quickly repackaged the beautiful rings I received as an anniversary gift and also enclosed my original wedding rings. I immediately took the package to the post office and sent it back to Sack. Inside the package was a brief note telling him how upset I was about making his mother the priority in our marriage. I went on to tell him that his being six years older than me did not give him the right to discount me in decisions that affected both our futures merely because I was young. I restated that I did not want to be married to him any longer, and said I was done!

After sending my note ending my marriage, I sulked for over a week, embraced every angry thought that entered my head, and found myself in a really bad funk. *How dare he reenlist without including me in that decision!* Ordinarily, I would pray and have a serious talk with God about my troubles, but this time, I just couldn't pray through my anger. I felt helpless—like I had just been robbed. I wasn't exactly sure of what I should do next, but I desperately needed a soft place to fall, so I called my old friend, Shoff, for consolation.

When Shoff answered the phone, he was shocked to hear from me although he said it was a very pleasant surprise. I poured out my heart to him. After listening intently to my sob stories of how my marriage was over, how inconsiderate my husband had been toward me, the mean things he said to me, and his decision to reenlist without discussing it with me, Shoff suggested we meet for a bite to eat so I could get everything off my chest. I was an emotional mess, but I agreed to meet him the next day. My thinking was so focused on needing a friend to lean on until I just didn't think anything negative about seeing my old beau again.

I had recently bought a new car the week before all the marital drama began, and I knew Shoff would be pleased to see it because he was a car enthusiast. I drove to his apartment around noon to pick him up. The new-car smell was still there after a week, and as Shoff sat down on the new seats, he commented on how nice my 1966 Chevy Malibu was. He especially loved its blue color. He said it went well with my eyes. I told him I wasn't hungry, so we drove around for about an hour. *I let him drive so I could continue talking.* Because I was talking so much and paying little attention to where he was driving, I didn't notice when the car stopped. As I looked around, I realized we were parked in a wooded area with not a soul in sight. Since it was still daylight outside, I gave no thought to it being an awkward situation for me.

Shoff crawled into the backseat and made himself comfortable, all the while listening to me ramble on and on about my woes. I told him about everything—even the part about my husband telling me a day before the wedding that a former girlfriend was expecting his child, who, by the way, was born five days after we were married. As I talked, a part of me secretly wondered why Shoff was so attentive to me. But at no time did he appear to be anything but concerned about the pain I was trying to talk myself through.

Finally, when I calmed down and was breathing normally again, Shoff said that he was happy that we were still friends and really glad that I called to confide in him. I felt comfortable sharing my situation with him and continued with the conversation. After about an hour of talking across the front seat, he suggested I climb in the back of the car with him, take off my shoes, get comfortable, and wiggle my toes out of the back window like he was doing. So I did.

The personality I saw in Shoff that day was not the one I used to know. He was a kinder, gentler soul. Perhaps he too had matured over the past nineteen months since our breakup. Whoever that person who was peering at me through those warm, caring eyes was certainly someone I wasn't in a rush to get away from. Not only did he listen to my ramblings, but I listened to his stories also. Turns out, Shoff enlisted into the army as a paratrooper after I called off our wedding in the fall of 1964. It was just coincidental my distress call to him on May 20, 1966, came while he was home on a thirty-day leave.

Several more hours passed, and we were still talking and laughing. I had propped myself against his chest and never actually realized that he was holding me. I guess his strong arms around me felt so natural and comfortable that I didn't think about those gestures in a romantic way. However, when Shoff told me that he *still*, and always would, love me despite the fact that I chose to walk out of his life, I thought for a split second I had made the wrong decision to not marry him but quickly reassured myself that I had done the right thing of not going through with our wedding. I enjoyed lots of laughter with Shoff when we were together. I never had laughter with my husband. During the time I was spending with my ex-fiancé, it quickly dawned on me just how blind I had been to what was really important in matters of the heart—instead, I had only focused on moving out of my parents' house instead of trying to understand what real love is!

12

A Cheating Heart

> *Delight of lust is gross and brief*
> *And weariness treads on desire.*
>
> —Charles Perrault (1628-1703)

By now, it was early evening as my rendezvous with Shoff continued. Up until that moment, we hadn't realized the chemistry we once had for each other was still there. I told Shoff that although we didn't get married, I'd always have a special place in my heart for him. Then Shoff gently kissed me on the back of my neck and I didn't pull away or ask him to stop. Feeling the closeness of his face and his gentle kisses gave me tingly sensations that I hadn't felt with him before. It had been twelve long months since I had been intimate with a man, and Shoff still knew how to push my buttons. I quickly forgot that I was legally married to Sack and gave my full attention to all the affection and comfort Shoff gave me that warm May afternoon in the backseat of my car. As we freely surrendered ourselves to each other, I quickly forgot about everything and everyone.

It still escapes me why I wasn't consumed with guilt over those intimate moments I spent with Shoff; I have no words to describe the unexplainable emotional calm I felt inside after my rendezvous with him. Days turned into weeks that I had not answered any of my husband's letters. Although I had made up my mind that if I really did end my marriage to Sack, going back to Shoff was not an option for me because our relationship was purely a lustful one. And I knew that was not the basis on which to build a solid marriage.

One Sunday afternoon late in June, I tried to write Sack a letter. Neither my heart nor my head was in the task, but I pushed myself anyway. As I kept trying to find words to fill up one page, I felt like it was really a wasted effort. I kept getting distracted by a constant itch on my breasts. After the scratching didn't help, I raised my blouse and looked to see what was causing the itching. I thought something had bitten me, or I had a rash. To my amazement, I noticed my breasts were fuller, and there were tiny holes in my nipple; so I squeezed my right breast, and out came a milky substance. Immediately, I had a gnawing suspicion that I might be pregnant—for real! The memory of the time I spent with Shoff six weeks ago rushed full speed into my head. I thought to myself, *Oh! Jesus, I'm pregnant. What am I going to do now?*

It was pointless to second-guess myself. After all, I *was* quite fertile since it had been over a year since I was sexually active. However, the fact that I could be pregnant bolstered my resolve to stop feeling sorry for myself, but see this situation through—no matter what.

For a split second, I had flashbacks of the horror I experienced on April 23, 1963, when my mother tied me to Daddy's bed for that abortion; but I quickly repressed that pain because *this time*, things would be very different. I vowed that I would protect this child's life with my very own, and no one would ever again violate me again. More importantly, no amount of shame I would face for the choice I made which brought me to that situation could justify not having my baby.

After recovering from the shock that I might be pregnant with Shoff's child, I summoned the energy to finish writing the letter to Sack and continued to sit at my desk stunned. Overwhelming thoughts raced through my head like crazy. The first thing I had to do was to see a doctor and confirm my suspicion. The next thing I focused on was how I would break this news to my husband. Even though I had written Sack that I didn't want to be married to him anymore, my situation surely made divorce a certainty now. Clearly, my infidelity could be grounds for Sack to have a slam dunk case.

I quickly got a hold of myself and vowed that I would stand up to all the flack that might come my way because of what I had done. Having this child was an absolute. I was fully prepared for the consequences of my choice to be intimate with Shoff. This time, my mother would not interfere with this life as long as God kept breath in my body.

I saw a doctor that same week. He confirmed that I was six weeks pregnant. I thought to myself, *I actually conceived this child on May 20*. I decided to not tell anyone about this pregnancy, not even Dee. I intended to move out of my parents' home long before Sack was due back in six months, especially since I'd be showing by that time. I totally believed my marriage would not survive my infidelity even if we could patch up the other issues between us. I felt it would take an extraordinary man to forgive my indiscretion and stay married to me. There was no way I would *not* have this baby. The life inside me was more important to me than whether my marriage could survive or not. I mentally prepared myself for a rough road ahead.

Although I hadn't settled it in my mind exactly how I would tell Sack about my baby, I knew it was inevitable that he would find out but decided not to write him a Dear John letter while he was in Vietnam because I felt that would be cruel. Shoff had returned to his army base in North Carolina, so I didn't contact him either to let him know I was pregnant with his child. He was the least of my worries at that point. The next day, I began looking for an apartment so I could move out of my parents' house.

I stopped writing my husband eight letters a week after his news to me in May that he was extending his tour of duty by six months for his mother's sake. Sack's letters to me were full of questions why I hadn't written him. They also contained many apologies for the poor way he had handled the allotment and medical insurance situations with his mom. They were also full of promises to be a better husband once he returned from Vietnam. Sack pleaded in his letters for me not to leave him and said we could work things out when he came home. He insisted that he loved me, repeatedly asked for my forgiveness, and assured me that everything would be just fine once he got home. Regardless of his pleas, I avoided responding to Sack in the slow trickle of letters I resumed sending. However, I decided not tell him about the baby while he was still in the war because I wanted to preserve his dignity even though I harbored unforgiveness toward him for the emotional abuse he had put me through.

I found myself a lovely apartment across town from my family and moved in within three weeks after learning I was pregnant. This was the first step, so I thought, to handling my situation. I totally believed I could take care of myself; I had a good job with medical insurance that would cover the hospital expenses when I gave birth, and thanks to my mother, I certainly knew a lot about the domestic side of keeping a home.

I did, however, write in one of my letters to Sack that I had moved into an apartment but gave him the excuse that I had been really busy as the reason for the slow trickle of mail. He sensed my pulling away from him because the next letter I received from him was a shocker: it said he was coming home in three weeks! Apparently, when I sent the wedding rings back and told him I didn't want to be married to him anymore, he went to his CO and withdrew his papers to extend his tour of duty to save his marriage.

The impact of that news gave me a headache, and I immediately had to lie down. Now my goose was really cooked because I didn't have a plan ready how I would tell him about my infidelity, my pregnancy, and my intention to get a divorce! This was a really big *Oh! Jesus* moment for me, and it was not a pretty situation!

I have learned that . . .

- **Experience is the result of my mistakes.**

    I shrugged off my responsibility for some of the bad choices I made. At the cost of many mistakes, I learned through experience and slowly gained strength, courage, and confidence from each of them.

- **All pain is the same—it hurts.**

    Pain is to be expected in life and is more bottomless than thought. I experienced a lot of pain in my early life—some by my own hand, some by the hands of others. Through it all, I did not give up on myself regardless of the stormy circumstance. I have learned that forgiveness is an absolute although it took me almost a lifetime to learn that.

- **God is sovereign and merciful.**

    Throughout those years of despair, pain, and hypocrisy, God did good things daily for me that I didn't deserve. He showered me with favor and mercy. His bigness was at work in my life although I couldn't consciously appreciate it. I also didn't fully understand where my grit came from during my challenges, but now that I am older and wiser, I know God was holding on to me tightly.

- **Fear can disguise itself as confidence.**

    Being afraid comes with the province of being human. It sneaks up on us at the weirdest times, though it can also overwhelm us and mimic confidence. Sometimes fear consumed me as a result of my poor choices or my laziness or my lack of knowledge. Sometimes I could have tried harder or sought God more earnestly. Many of my heartaches could have been avoided if I was smarter, or more patient with myself. Despite myself, the love of God embraced and sustained me even when I was afraid and thought I was just being confident.

Section III

The Red Road

Passion impels our deeds;
Ideology supplies the explanations.

Mason Cooley (1927-2002)

I did not see that the tragedy I suffered early in my life was the catalyst that turned me into the hip slingin' daughter of Satan that I became. Promiscuity was an art form for me, and men were insignificant creatures I viewed as grass and I, the lawn mower. I did not, and could not, fully comprehend God's infinite love for me during my destructive behavior while traveling over the red road of my rainbow. However, there was a divine thread woven into my life that protected me from myself; that thread was my savior, Jesus Christ.

13

Deceive Me If You Can

*Things and actions are what they are,
And the consequences of them will be what they will be:
Why then should we desire to . . . deceive.*

—Bishop Joseph Butler (1692-1752)

As the time grew closer to when my husband would be coming home from the war and finding out I was in a family way, I wrestled with mixed emotions how my life would dramatically change when that truth came out. I was in a quandary how to best handle the situation. On one hand, I thought my message was clear when I sent my wedding rings back, telling Sack that I didn't want the marriage to continue. On the other hand, my message seemingly didn't register because he wrote me back, insisting and promising to do everything he could to make our marriage work when he came home from the war. Although I had a serious dilemma on my hands, I figured I had two choices. My first choice—door number 1—and the most difficult, was telling him the truth and accepting the consequences that would follow. The second choice—door number 2—was easier to execute albeit the most deceptive. That being not fess up, making the situation benefit me by pretending I conceived immediately after he arrived home. The second plan would basically buy me some time to prepare for the consequences I'd face after giving birth, especially since I would have difficulty explaining a full-term nine-month baby as a seven-month preemie.

I subconsciously convinced myself that getting pregnant while my husband was in Vietnam was not an act of retaliation against him for (1) not telling me about his paternity issue until a day before our wedding and (2) being accused of concealing little Marian as my child. However, deep down, I suspected the magnitude of those two things did fuel a spirit of rebellion inside me to hurt him back. I do know I acted recklessly with Shoff the day we spent together parked on that secluded hill. What I didn't understand was why I was having so much inner turmoil over confessing my sins, taking my lumps, and walking away from my marriage. No doubt, fear and a very strong root of pride had taken hold of me.

July 14, 1966, my husband arrived home from Vietnam. It was a hot summer day, and I was very nervous about seeing him after having been apart for fourteen months. I picked Sack up from the Greyhound bus station in my new car. I still remember his infamous one-thousand-watt smile that day; he had perfect pearly white teeth and he looked wonderful in his uniform. When Sack saw me, he immediately rushed up and picked me up, spun me around, and excitedly told me the surprising news that his tour of duty was over and that he was out of the army for good. That means he was home to stay! I tried to hide the look of shock on my face as I was having another *Oh! Jesus* moment. Hearing that news should have bolstered my resolve to tell him the truth about my infidelity and that I was expecting a child. But it didn't. Instead, I kept quiet and waited for a better time to bring up the matter.

Next I drove him to visit his mom and some family members, and our final stop was to my mother's house. I was glad about all the stops we made before going home because I was still grappling with how I would tell Sack my bad news. I tried to smile and exude an excited personality, but it was hard for me to camouflage my uneasiness. We finally arrived at the apartment late that evening. Sack was quite pleased with how beautiful the apartment looked and complimented me over and over on what a great job I had done decorating the place. He continued to talk for hours, going on and on about the war and his faith in God while in Vietnam. He even showed me a pocket Bible my mother had given him before he shipped out. He added that she told him to read Psalms 91 every day if he could. And he did.

As it grew later that night, I knew sleep was the last thing on Sack's mind. Every time that I'd start to make my confession, he started a new topic of conversation telling me how good it was to be home, how much he loved and missed me, and that he was glad we were finally together. He seemed so happy, which made it even harder for me to get up the courage to ruin his mood on his first day home. I felt so much compassion for Sack until I just couldn't get up the courage to make my confession to him that night. So I took the coward's approach and didn't tell him about my situation because it just seemed easier to simply go with the flow and keep my secret a little longer. Sack was so excited to be with me until he never even noticed how cold and distant I was to his touch. Although I was numb inside with guilt and didn't want the inevitable physical intimacy that was fast approaching, I submitted to his connubial needs. It was a *long* night.

His appetite for me finally subsided after about a week, and I was very concerned about the vigorous sexual activity he had put me through being harmful to my baby. Ironically, Sack joked about *surely making me pregnant "this time."* After he said that, the proverbial light bulb went on in my head, and I was crystal clear on what I would do about my situation—I chose door number 2.

A month later, Sack landed a great job and quickly settled into his new lifestyle as a civilian and wage earner. I too adjusted to the role of wife, doing all the housekeeping chores as well as going to work five days a week and meeting the job demands that came with working at the National Security Agency. About six weeks after my husband had been home, the plot of my charade thickened. One Saturday morning, I felt nauseated and quickly bolted out of bed into the bathroom to throw up. I knew it was morning sickness because I was now three months along and could no longer delay coming up with a plan of action.

After cleaning myself up, I looked around and noticed Sack standing in the doorway of the bathroom with a concerned look on his face. He asked me if I was okay. To which I answered, "I feel much better after throwing up. I wonder if I'm pregnant." That was my coup de théâtre. I only wanted to get through the few months left, and I gave no thought to what the end result would be to my ill-timed lie once my baby was born. That next week, I told my husband I saw the doctor, and it was official. I was pregnant! He did not have a reaction, one way or another, to my announcement but just looked at me sort of weird like. Now that he knew I was expecting a baby, I felt a huge sense of relief from the pressure I had put on myself. I actually convinced my subconscious psyche that he *was* the father although the real truth was foremost in my mind.

After several months, we began arguing and bickering about almost everything. I discovered that he was very controlling and did not like it when I regularly pushed back against his demands. He quickly discovered that "meek," "passive," and "subservient" were not a part of my DNA. Our fights were never about my housekeeping—I generally kept the house neat and clean—nor did we fight about money. We fought about religion and sex. Let me explain. The guilt that I carried inside about the deception I was enacting drove me to become very spiritual, which I used to assuage my guilt over the situation I had created. I joined a local Pentecostal church, whose legalistic doctrines influenced me in ways that caused more conflict in the marriage. Since my feigned affection had been a ruse, I began refusing my husband's approaches for intimacy because I had no desire to pretend any longer since I found the exercise boring. Sack would get so angry with me when I would collapse onto the floor. The weight of my baby resting on my pelvis caused me debilitating pain throughout my pregnancy. Remember that childhood hip injury I sustained jumping out of a window on a dare? Well it reared its ugly head during my pregnancy as my belly grew larger. Sack thought I was being dramatic to discourage him from approaching me for sex. He was very insensitive to the hip pain I coped with and that made me dislike him even more.

One night while we were lying in bed arguing over my refusal to be intimate with him, Sack got so angry that he hopped out of bed, picked up the side of the mattress, and literally threw a pregnant me out of the bed onto the floor! Then he climbed back in bed and announced that if I didn't put out, I could not sleep on *his* bed. So I picked myself up off the floor, walked to the living room, and slept on the couch. He soon learned that his fits of rage got him nowhere.

Five months into the marriage charade, it was crystal clear to me that our relationship was in shambles. Another memorable fight happened one Sunday morning as I was getting ready for church. Because Sack was vehemently opposed to me going to the church I had aligned myself with, he was determined I was not going to their services that day. We argued like animals, neither one listening to the other. He then pushed me out of his way ('cause I was all up in his face), went to my closet, gathered up all my maternity clothes, and threw them onto the front lawn from the second-floor patio of our apartment building. Next he went to my car and disabled it from starting by pulling out the wires in the distributor cap.

After Sack angrily left the house, I managed to take my half-dressed pregnant self outside to pick up every piece of my clothing that had been thrown onto the front lawn. Neighbors were peering at me through their windows, but I kept gathering my things. After I brought everything back upstairs, I found an outfit that wasn't soiled and dressed myself for church. Since my husband had disabled my car before, I was fully prepared to fix it. (What he didn't know was after he pulled that trick a previous time, my Dad helped me get going by giving me a spare set of distributor wires and a detailed diagram on how to insert each wire back into the distributor cap so my car could start.) I opened my locked glove compartment and took out the diagram and spare wires. Within ten minutes, I had reassembled my distributor, cranked my car up, and drove to church. Needless to say, when Sack returned home and saw that my car and I were gone, he never tried that stunt again.

Because we argued most of the time, I wanted peace of mind more than I wanted to be married, so I decided to leave my husband and emphatically told him so. Oftentimes, I would quote Proverbs 25:24 as the biblical justification for leaving him: "It is better to dwell in the corner of the housetop, than with a brawling woman and in a wide house." Naturally, he blamed my church for putting that idea in my head and using that scripture out of context. I called my Dad and asked him to come get me. I packed some clothes and went back to my parents' home.

Dad had warned my husband just before our wedding ceremony that if he couldn't treat me right, he needed to bring me back home. Since I regularly bad-mouthed Sack to my parents, Dad didn't think twice about helping me leave him. Sack called every day, begging me to come back. He promised not to bother me for sex if I didn't want him to and agreed not to fuss with me about my church attendance. He just wanted me back in his life. His pleadings eventually wore me down, and I agreed to go back to him.

My husband and I were both hypocrites whose lives together were mired in omissions, lies, and deceptions. There was no way trust and honesty could flourish in that marriage environment. However, I was more concerned about the soon-coming birth of my baby than I was about my marriage.

It was an especially hard time for Sack; our marriage was in trouble, and his mother had fallen ill and was not expected to live much longer. Although I knew in my heart of hearts that my marriage was not foundationally sound, I was sensitive to his situation, supportive of his family, and completely understanding of his long days at the hospital by his mom's bedside. Sadly, a month before I gave birth, my mother-in-law died. My husband handled her loss better than I expected him to, and he never let me see him cry.

Following my mother-in-law's death, the home front was calm for a while. I was consumed with my approaching due date and how I would deal with a February birth that was not supposed to happen until April, which would be nine months from when my husband came home. But the reality of not telling my husband the truth early on about my pregnancy frightened me more than I thought it would.

Even though I knew my baby was due in February, I continued working as though I was due in April. Although I was actually in my ninth month, I squeezed my big belly behind the steering wheel of my car and drove forty-five miles to and from Fort Meade every day. My office planned to give me a baby shower on February 17. However, I went into labor at 9:30 PM on February 10.

Sack worked the evening shift and didn't get home until around midnight. That meant I had about two hours to get my story together as to why I was having pain. My labor progressed, and I was having contractions every twenty minutes. So when Sack got home, I told him *I fell up the stairs on my belly* and was in a lot of pain after the jolt. Even though that lie sounded like a good one to me, I thought it would get me some sympathy but Sack just looked at me and mumbled how tired he was. Next he took a shower and went to bed. Before falling off to sleep, he told me to wake him if the pains didn't stop; then he rolled over and quickly started snoring.

The hours rolled by slowly, and my pains became more intense. My belly was really large, and several friends guessed that my baby would weigh at least seven pounds at birth. I pondered some of the consequences facing me once Sack saw my child, especially if my baby didn't look like him or was too big to *pass* as a preemie. Would he immediately know he was not the father? Would he act ugly? Make a scene at the hospital? Or would we have a civil discussion about the matter and come to a mutual agreement about what we would do?

When Saturday morning finally arrived, my pains were ten minutes apart. I had suffered alone all night but I knew it was almost time to give birth, so I called the doctor; and he told me to go to the hospital right away. At 12:28 PM on that sunny but cold February day, my beautiful daughter was born. She weighed seven pounds, six and a half ounces, was perfect, and healthy. She was also the spitting image of her Dad—the biological one, that is—and to my amazement, she had my husband's right dimple and trademark pointed left ear! I named her Pamela.

Within minutes of seeing my baby girl's perfect little face, Sack doted on her and never said a word to me about how large she was (to be a preemie) or that she didn't look like either of us. I knew in my heart that he knew she was not his child, but it was very apparent to me that nothing else mattered to him at that moment than his new family. Three days later, I went home with my little angel and began life as a new mom.

14

Nothing Beats a Try . . . But

'Tis a lesson you should heed, Try, try again.
If at first you don't succeed, Try, try again.

—W. E. Hickson (1803-1870)

My life now had a new focus since the birth of my daughter. The concentrated energy I placed on her needs temporarily insulated me from the discontent I felt in my marriage. Perhaps the root of my discontent was acting as though we were a happy family when, in truth, I was uncomfortable with the life of pretense I tried hard to make believable. Little did I know Sack was completely aware of the truth that Pamela was not his biological child. At all costs, he opted not to make it an issue between us. He obviously had forgiven me and was happy with our family unit. I guess, for him, the situation was not a deal breaker.

Once I realized Sack wanted our family to stay intact, I tried really hard to make my marriage to him work. More than anything else, I wanted to be a mother. Now that I had a beautiful daughter to care for, I thought my baby would make the wife task easier. But it didn't.

Learning how to juggle the responsibilities of a career, motherhood, chores, and wifedom were not as easy as I made it look. I passed my six-week postnatal examination and went back to work. Aside from the fact that it was difficult for me to tear myself away from my new baby girl, it was doubly hard for me to get up every morning and get us both out the door for the brutal schedule I was on. My biggest challenge was getting to work on time for a 7:15 AM shift. My morning routine, driving from home to the babysitter and then to my job, was a daily total of forty-five miles each way.

At that time, I had been working for the government for a little over two and a half years; six months of which was in a new position as clerk typist for an older retired army general. I made a good salary with reasonable benefits. The work was easy, not overwhelming nor demanding. However, I struggled with the rigors of new motherhood for seven months to get out of the house by 6:00 AM so I could be at my desk by 7:15 AM. Hard as I tried, the best I could do was arrive at 7:20 AM. The general was adamant about punctuality and decided to straighten me out for showing up five minutes late for work every day!

One morning, after taking off my coat and sitting down at my desk, Dr. Straw walked up to me and sternly told me to take one hour of annual leave each time I was five minutes late getting to work—starting with that day. I looked up at him and offered a very sincere apology while sharing with him the fact that I had been staying an extra ten minutes each day to offset my five-minute lateness. I tried convincing him I was trying hard to not be late for work, but making the adjustment as a new mother was taking me longer than I had imagined. I asked him if he would be willing to work with me a little while longer and let me use leave on a cumulative basis instead of taking one hour daily for being five minutes tardy. I thought the general would cut me some slack since I was a good worker, dependable and conscientious. His answer was an emphatic no! That was the day I discovered something interesting about myself: I was stubborn, prideful, and just as unyielding as the general and felt compelled to challenge him.

I knew it was my responsibility to get to work on time, and it was irrelevant to management that I was a twenty-year-old new mother. But as a firm believer that one is accountable for one's actions, I had to make a hard choice concerning the well-being of my baby. I was already getting up at 5:00 AM so Pamela and I could be out the door by 6:00 AM to get her to day care. Sometimes, traffic flowed, and forty-five minutes was enough time for me to drive to Fort Meade; other times traffic didn't flow. I made the decision to not stress myself out anymore because I didn't want to get up any earlier than I already was. So I took a deep breath, put a piece of paper into my typewriter, and typed my letter of resignation, giving Dr. Straw two weeks' notice. I read my letter carefully, signed it, walked into his office, handed it to him, turned, and went back to my desk.

That was the day I grew my sea legs as a bona fide risk taker. But deep inside of me, there was a certainty about my work situation that made me know everything would work out just fine. I completely understood that my boss believed penalizing me for tardiness was the way to make me get to work on time. I also understood that his military background trained him to only see black and white in given situations, and exercising flexibility with me was not an option.

> *I've come to understand and accept that life does have gray areas; every situation is not always black and white nor is there always a simple remedy for those gray areas. That's why being open-minded, flexible, and adaptable, can be your best decision-making tools.*

What happened next surprised me. The general came up to my desk with my resignation letter in his hand. His face was as white as a sheet. He looked at me and asked, "Are you sure you want to do this?"

To which I replied, "Yes, I'm sure. You see, the choices you gave me were non-negotiable, and I chose the path of least resistance." I added, "Since I am a new mother, my first priority is to my child—I am not willing to get my baby up any earlier than 5:00 AM just so I can come to *this* job when I can find another one that will have a later starting time." At that point, his whole demeanor changed as he asked me to reconsider my decision to leave admitting that good help, like me, was hard to find. Dr. Straw reminded me I was only three months short of reaching career status with the government, and as a new parent, I needed my job; but he never addressed a work-around plan for my five-minute tardiness issue. He actually looked sorry for pushing me to that limit. I'm sure he never expected me, as a black woman, to challenge him that way. Nonetheless, I graciously refused to change my mind.

Looking back at that day, I admit that my pride was in control of my decision to leave the general's office, and I was not willing to forgive him for what I thought was inflexibility. I believe that was the day my pride created the "I don't have to take this" attitude in me. It never occurred to me to be concerned or somewhat frightened about quitting my job on the spot like that. Somehow, I had no doubt in my heart that my *best friend* would bless me with another one—and a better one at that!

When I arrived home from work, I told my husband I had given my two-week notice to quit my job. He looked at me like I had three heads, never asked what happened or why; but he just flipped out and blurted, "Are you crazy?" I told him I wasn't worried because God would open a door and give me another job. Two weeks later, I ended my government job with the general on a Friday and started a new job that Monday with the housing authority where my shift started at 8:30 AM. From that day on, Sack became a believer that I would always land on my feet because of my faith.

As the marriage continued to deteriorate, we hit another rocky patch just before Christmas, and I became more determined to somehow escape the bed of thorns I allowed myself to lie in. I left Sack for the third time. I rented a small apartment in the city for $14 a week. Admittedly, my leaving Sack and going back to him repeatedly was getting really old by now. I wanted to break the cycle I kept falling into. Like always, Sack worried me every day with phone calls, pleading for Pamela and me to come back home. Several months later, I went back to him one more time.

When Pamela turned one, I knew the marriage could not survive, but I didn't want her to be an only child. That's when I decided to have another baby. Right after going back to my husband, I conceived my son on May 6 of 1968—the very same week I moved back with Sack. This pregnancy was much easier for me. It sure helped having prior experience as a mommy to a busy toddler because I received no help from my husband. However, my mother was extremely attached to my Pamela and insisted on babysitting her while I worked or whenever I needed care for her while I ran an errand. Not only did I work a full-time job, but also a part-time evening job downtown as a check processor in a local bank.

The proverbial straw that broke the camel's back came one cold and snowy Thursday night late in January of 1969. I was on my way home from my second job after picking up my daughter around 11:30 PM from my mother's house when it began to sleet; the streets were ice covered and treacherous. As I navigated down a hill on my way home, I hit an ice patch, and my car slid into a parked car. Another car coming down that same icy hill slid into the back of my car, knocking my sleeping toddler onto the floor. Before I could safely get us out of the car, we were hit two more times. Fortunately, they were not hard crashes and we didn't get hurt.

The driver who hit my car helped me safely walk on the icy street to a nearby house and carried my daughter for me. When the gentleman saw I was pregnant, he asked me when was my baby due. He nearly freaked out when I told him, "Any day now." Once we were safely inside the home, I called Sack to tell him we had been in an accident and asked him to come and get us because I didn't want to continue driving home in the storm. I was shocked at his response after telling him about my accident. Sack was actually angry with me for waking him up but more agitated that he had to get dressed and come out in the cold to pick us up. I was livid with him for being angry about the accident and his callous disregard for my well-being, especially with me being nine months pregnant with his child—his biological child.

That night, his behavior solidified my decision to get out of that marriage as soon as I could after giving birth. The next day, I called my Dad to tell him about my accident and put him on notice that I would need his help *one last time* to assist me in getting another apartment and some furniture. I told him I was leaving Sack for good, and I was never, ever coming back. Dad had never heard me say *I was never coming back*. As always, he assured me he would be there for me when I needed him.

Two weeks after the accident, I gave birth to a beautiful blue-eyed baby boy on February 12, 1969, and named him Paisley after my Dad. He weighed seven pounds, thirteen ounces and had the cutest little face you've ever seen. Sack was excited about having a son and expected that he would have his name. However, his excitement was short-lived when he found out that did not happen. *I had no intention of naming my son after a husband who abused me.* I named my son after my Dad because it was *he* who had been my safe harbor throughout the tumultuous times of my marriage. (Naming my son after my Dad was my tribute to him and the beginning of me trying to forgive him for his part in the tragic loss of my first child.)

If there was any lingering doubt in my mind that there was salvageable life left in my marriage to Sack, that question was clearly answered for me when he drove my (our) son and me home from the hospital.

After I told Sack I had named the baby after my Dad, he was incensed. He was so angry that I thought he would hit me. The rage that seethed inside him was indescribable. Earlier that morning, a hospitality employee delivered my baby's hospital pictures to me just before I was discharged to go home. While I was in the restroom getting dressed to go home, unbeknownst to me, Sack took the envelope with my son's pictures and tore every one of them to shreds. *Had it not been for the one picture I had put in my wallet earlier, I would not have a newborn picture of Little Pais.*

Sack ranted, raved, and berated me the entire ride as he drove me home from the hospital. When we arrived at our townhouse, he opened the front door and pitched my overnight bag inside while pushing me into the house as I tightly held on to our three-day-old son. He slammed the door behind us, angrily drove off, and left me alone the entire day to fend for myself. I immediately called my sister for help and explained to her what had just happened. I asked if she would come over and help me get situated on the first floor so I wouldn't have to go up and down the stairs. We lived in a two-story townhouse. My sister brought my mother and two-year-old Pamela with her. She and Mom helped me make bottles of formula for Pais, set up a bed for me on the first floor, and conveniently arranged all the baby supplies I needed to function for a few days. Sack came home the next morning and didn't talk to me for three days.

Sheer determination to have a better life for myself, especially peace of mind, fueled my resolve to do something about my home life. Every time I looked at my husband, I felt nothing but contempt for him. Realizing just how cold and uncaring Sack had become helped me clearly see that a divorce was inevitable.

During the weeks preceding my medical release to return to work, I diligently put a plan together for my final exodus. I interviewed for and landed a higher-paying job with the railroad, secured an apartment, bought some furniture (with my Dad's help, of course), and arranged for a move-in date. Six weeks to the day after Paisley's birth, I moved out and left Sack for the *last time*. There would be no coming back! I left him the entire contents in our house except for the children's and my personal things.

I tightly held my two-year-old daughter's little hand and safely carried my six-week-old baby boy in my other arm as I closed the door to the townhouse and my world with Sack. I put my children into my car and drove off into the sunset to my new life as a single mother of a toddler and a brand-new 6-week old baby. I never looked back nor ever went back to Sack after that day.

15

On My Own

Whatever brawls disturb the street,
There should be peace at home.

—Isaac Watts (1674-1748)

Living on my own surpassed even *my* imaginings now that the brawling and bickering with my husband, Sack, were out of my life. I knew it would not be easy as a single parent of two toddlers, but I was determined to be a good mother at any cost, and working hard was second nature for me. Dad cosigned for me to get the furniture I needed to set up my apartment, and I assured him I would keep up the payments.

The day my new furniture was delivered felt like Christmas. As my new sofa came through the front door of my newly rented apartment—along with lamps, tables, bunk beds for the children, a dining room set, and bedroom for me—I was a giggly mess from sheer joy. The smell of new furniture permeated my house for weeks! Life was good, and I thanked God daily for where He blessed me to be!

I actually found joy in the transition out of the role as wife to single mom. I no longer had to hear "What's for dinner?" or be reminded there were no more clean underwear in the drawer. Without a doubt, one of my biggest pleasures was stretching myself sideways in my bed and no longer fighting over the bedcovers! Ironically, it was during this time that I discovered the latent decorator inside of me; and before long, my walls were splashed with vivid colors from the many wallpapering experiments I tried. My new home with my two children was cozy and very comfortable.

My workweek was not too stressful; and before long, I had settled nicely into the daily routine at the end of the day of picking up my children from day care, coming home, preparing and feeding them dinner, giving baths, and doing our bedtime *thing*—sharing lots of hugs and kisses, helping them say their prayers, and tucking each one into bed. Once they were asleep, I would do laundry, iron, or simply enjoy some quiet time. By no means am I saying that taking care of two toddlers was easy because it wasn't. I guess I just made it look easy. I now know that my determination to shield my children from most of life's ugliness was what fueled me to keep pushing.

Yes, definitely, there were times I felt overwhelmed as a mother. I sometimes cried myself to sleep when I felt consumed by all that I had to do to keep things running smoothly for my babies and me. I often called my sister Dee and dumped on her. She, in turn, always listened to my whining and sometimes commiserated with me by saying, "Girl, I know what you're saying—it ain't easy!" She did her best to comfort me. At that time, my sister didn't have children of her own to know what I was going through or how I was really feeling. Occasionally, I would have a pity party and feel sorry for myself. There were also times when I would fuss with God about how hard my life was, like when there was no food in the fridge or how it was commonplace that my paychecks didn't cover the monthly demands on my budget. It never failed; every time I'd find myself in that funk, a little voice deep inside my soul would remind me of all the good stuff that filled my life—like having two healthy children, a job, a roof over my head, a car that ran well, good health, a good mind, and people who cared about me. Slowly, I would refocus on my blessings and crawl out of my valley.

One day while grocery shopping, I met a fella whom I shall call OW. We struck up a conversation in the produce aisle. I was impressed with his strong personality. I had never met such a bold man before. He quickly asked me if he could call me sometimes. OW was eleven years older than I was; but I quickly found myself attracted to his aggressive personality—not aggressive as in abusive, but aggressive as in a no-nonsense personality. Perhaps I was attracted to older men because I wanted masculine comfort like that of a father. I didn't question the *why* of my attraction, but I just went with the flow. OW rarely smiled but often made me laugh to the point of tears with his dry humor. He taught me how to stand up for myself in matters that required absolute confidence. My mother told Sack that I was seeing someone, and that piece of news was all he needed to start harassing me again. Whenever Sack called to see how the children were doing, he would nag me about us being a family again and beg me to come back to him.

About six weeks before my birthday in July, Sack began stalking me by coming to my apartment on his way home from his 4:00-11:00 PM shift every Friday. Once at my front door, he would turn his back to the door, knock on the door standing backward, and just stand there waiting on me to open the door. His knocking would go on for about fifteen minutes. Most nights, I'd jump out of bed terrified by his thunderous knocks, but I would not open my door or acknowledge him. This would usually happen around 1:00 AM on Friday nights. Fortunately, the neighbors in my apartment building didn't complain about Sack's weekly disruptions to their nighttime quiet.

The Friday night before my birthday, I sat up for the remainder of another disrupted night of sleep after Sack stopped knocking on my door. I was at the point of honest-to-God madness. I didn't know how to make him stop bothering me, but I also didn't want to open the door to see if I could reason with him either. I felt helpless and totally devastated because I didn't know what to do. Since Sack and I were still legally married, he probably felt he could make demands on me just as if we were living together as man and wife despite the fact that we had been separated for almost two years. And his regular conversations with my mother were only making matters worse; she gave him false hope about a reconciliation. Apparently, her news about me dating flipped Sack out and pushed his crazy button.

Sack returned the next day, Saturday (my birthday), and showed his natural butt. When he knocked on the door, I looked through the peephole and saw him holding up a birthday cake for me to see. I guess he thought it would be an incentive for me to open the door. He pleaded with me to let him in so he could celebrate my birthday with the children. I wasn't sure if the cake was a ruse or not, so for our safety, I decided to quickly leave my house. As quietly as I could, I gathered my two children, my purse, and keys; quietly unlocked my patio door; and carefully ran to my car to get out of there. The last thing I remember was Sack pounding on that door, screaming for me to open it.

I drove around town for about an hour and then went to Dee's apartment for refuge. We only lived four blocks from each other. She had bought cake and ice cream for me, so the children and I celebrated my birthday with her. The kids were getting restless because it was close to their bedtime, so we left Dee's and went home.

When I arrived at my front door, I noticed it had been forced open, and the wood around the lock was split. My heart immediately sank to my heels, and I could feel anxiety rising inside me. I didn't know whether Sack had broken into my apartment and was still inside waiting to hurt me, or he had just broken in to give me the birthday cake since I wouldn't open the door and let him in. I took a deep breath, put the children behind me to shield them, slowly pushed the door open, and went inside. I was horrified at what I saw. It was the worst birthday I could have imagined. Sack had vandalized my apartment, and the place looked like a war zone. My beautiful sofa set had long gashes from knife cuts, the curtains at the windows were also cut in shreds, the dining room table had long carved gashes, the china cabinet glass was broken, and all my good dishes were broken into pieces and strewn over the floor. My bedroom was also vandalized with deep gashes in my mattress, lamp shades, and curtains; and the countertop of each piece of bedroom furniture was destroyed with deep gashes in the wood. The only room in the apartment Sack didn't destroy was the children's room. There were no words to describe how angry I was. I immediately wanted to kill Sack.

I wasn't sure what to do, so the first person I called was OW. I told him what had happened, and he told me he would be at my house in twenty minutes and that I should sit tight until he got there. I made two other calls—one to my sister telling her about the vandalism and asking her to pick up and keep my children that night until I got the place cleaned up; the second call was to my mother telling her what "her Sack" had done. I also told her she better warn him because I was gonna hurt him! My four-year-old daughter, being the smart child that she was, questioned me why our house was a mess; so I told her a burglar had caused the damage and reassured her that everything was okay, that we were safe and that Aunt Dee was coming to pick her up so I could clean up the place.

When OW came in and saw my apartment, he mumbled something ugly about Sack and called him a few expletives. He asked if I had renter's insurance, and I assured him that I did. He stayed with me to help me get myself together from the shock of what had just happened. The confidence and assertiveness that OW displayed throughout my ordeal helped to override my anxieties. Somehow, I trusted him to get me through that situation. OW gave me explicit instructions what I was to say to the police. His parting words to me were, "Be sure and get a report number."

OW left, and I called the police to report the break-in. The police came to my apartment, looked around, and commented that it looked like a crime of passion because of the deep knife gashes throughout the place. They asked me if I had any idea who could have done that, and I said, "Perhaps it was my estranged husband of two years, but I didn't see him do it, so I can't say for sure." The police sat on a kitchen stool and wrote up the report. They gave me a long number and told me to make a report to my insurance company and give them that number. They left. I called OW, and he told me I should have a check-in about ten days if I get the paperwork done quickly. Two days later, Sack called like nothing had happened. I hung up on him and changed my phone number immediately.

Being able to produce receipts for everything that was damaged resulted in a better payout than I imagined because I did not have to guess at the value of my property. From that day on, I now keep receipts for everything I buy for at least seven years in case I need them. Just as OW said, I had my check in ten days. I took OW out for dinner at a really nice restaurant, and later that night, I thanked him *properly* for helping me get through that ordeal. I had the living room reupholstered, contracted a woodsmith to refinish all the damaged wood surfaces on my furniture, and purchased new curtains to replace the damaged ones at each window.

Let me back up for a second. A week after Sack vandalized my apartment, a really weird experience happened to me that gave me an unforgettable testimony about the saving grace of God. Each day that I looked at my apartment all cut up, unspeakable anger festered inside of me toward Sack. I decided to really hurt him the very next time he knocked on my door and turned his back. (To flawlessly execute the plan I came up with, I practiced my every move all week to ensure a perfect follow-through). That following Friday, at 1:00 AM like clockwork, Sack showed up at my door, turned backward and began knocking on my door. I gently stood up from my raggedy sofa, very quietly placed my left hand on the doorknob so he wouldn't hear any sounds as I opened the door. In my right hand was a butcher knife that I planned to thrust into Sack's back after quickly opening the door and striking him. But as I tried to turn the knob and follow through with my plan, I felt my whole body had become immobilized. I was not afraid, so I knew it was not fear that had paralyzed me. I was temporarily out of my mind with rage and ready to hurt Sack that night.

As I looked through the peephole of the door, I could see Sack standing backward. I kept trying to make myself move so I could turn that knob and replay that infamous *Psycho* scene in the hallway of my apartment. My body felt like it was encased in cement and I could only move my eyes. As I watched Sack begin walking away from the door and up the stairs, feeling returned to my body, and I quickly flung the door open and ran up the stairs behind him to stab him. In a split second, Sack turned around and saw a crazed lady [me] with a knife in her hand who had been pushed over the edge. He blocked my arm, and disarmed me just as I was about to push the knife into him. We struggled in the hallway, and the knife slipped through my hand, slicing it open. Sack saw all the blood, blurted out that it was my fault I got hurt and quickly ran up the steps. I called the police and had him arrested for assault. Sack never harassed me again with those thunderous late-night knocks on my door. He later told my mother that being arrested was the most humiliating thing that had ever happened to him, and he would not bother me again.

I am convinced it was the Holy Spirit that immobilized me that night to save me from myself. God knew my anger had reached a boiling point of no return, so He simply covered me with His loving arms long enough for Sack to walk away from my front door. It was God and God alone who saved Sack's life that night and kept me from committing murder.

Ironically, OW walked out of my life six months later. When I finally got him to take my call I asked why I hadn't seen or heard from him in over three weeks. He said he was falling in love with me, and he didn't want to be that emotionally attached to any woman. He also said it was nice while it lasted, said goodbye and hung up the phone! I was really hurt after OW said that. I hadn't done anything for him to just up and leave me so abruptly and I wasn't prepared for the breakup. After that happened, I promised myself I'd never be dumped by a boyfriend ever again.

I ran into OW about thirty years later on the subway. He was still single but had grown into an angry old man.

16

My Friend—Adversity

Adversity is the diamond dust Heaven polishes its jewels with.

—Robert Leighton

As my children grew older, my financial responsibilities increased, so I began looking for a higher-paying job. While combing through the Sunday want ads, one job caught my eye. It was a listing for an executive secretary at a local radio station. Since I still had a passion for the broadcasting industry, I decided to call the number in the ad to get more details about the position. I had a great interview and landed the job! The radio station was in dire need of someone to get them organized and manage the advertising that went on the broadcast log. The raise in pay was substantial from what I had been earning. The job was not difficult for me because I had a natural penchant for organizing *anything*. I learned a lot about the radio industry. Since I had been told I had a sexy voice, I was even allowed to male a few commercials just for the fun of it.

Within three months, I had whipped that office into a state of organized bliss. Whenever any of the announcers or vendors walked through the station, they couldn't believe that all the clutter and chaos were gone. It was a normal occurrence for recording celebrities to come to the station when the owner—James Brown (yes, the Godfather of Soul himself) was in town. I met several singing groups; I especially remember meeting the original O'Jays and the original Spinners. I also enjoyed dressing up and attending the lavish recording parties the station sometimes sponsored. Mr. Brown gave really first-class parties! At those parties, I'd get to sample lobster, filet mignon, and some out-of-this-world desserts. I didn't care much for the taste of alcohol, so I never got into drinking at those parties. Life was good for me during that time, and my kids wanted for nothing.

As an impressionable twenty-four-year-old who was trying to get comfortable with dating again, I would coyly bat my eyes at the fine male hunks that frequented the radio station just to see how much attention I could get from them. I was considered to be an attractive green-eyed caramel-colored little honey that could turn a few heads every now and then. Although I was very gullible and somewhat naïve about life despite all my experiences up to that point, I managed to make a good impression on most of the men I interacted with.

One afternoon in 1970, I heard a man's voice coming from the back of the studio that sounded like God speaking. The resonant tone of that announcer was so compelling until it sounded like liquid velvet! I knew all the announcers who worked at the station, but I had never heard *that voice* before, and I wanted to see who this person was. So I quietly walked down the hall to the sound room and peeked inside to see the face that went with that voice. To my amazement, the man sitting behind the mixing board looked like Adonis in the flesh! He was gorgeous! His skin was tan and smooth, and the thick mustache that outlined his plump lips drew me into his aura. There was an intriguing sexiness about him. He looked up from the board and caught me staring at him; our eyes locked, and I actually felt sparks fly. As I walked back to my office, I had to catch my breath, wipe sweat from my brow, and wait for my heart to stop racing. All I could say was, "Wow, who was that!"

I found out his name was RJ. He occasionally worked at the station making commercials, and I could not deny the attraction I felt to RJ. Going to work became more exciting after meeting RJ. I decided I wanted to get to know him. Although I was a bashful introvert, I enjoyed how RJ made me blush with his piercing looks and sensual propositions to go out with him. By the end of the summer, I was well aware of a powerful, and almost scary, chemistry between us. I toyed with the idea of a rendezvous with RJ, but I didn't act on my desire at that time because I wasn't sure if

I was ready to be that close to a man again, so I began practicing the art of *arm's-length flirting*.

I liked RJ a lot but only wanted him in small doses—like brief moments of laughter, flirting, or maybe a passing kiss. I kept things very light between us because I wasn't sure what I wanted to do with him. Although I was bashful, I knew I had a fickle nature and was certain I didn't want RJ as a boyfriend nor did I want to spend huge amounts of time with him, or any man for that matter. So I came up with the "teddy bear" arrangement and waited for the right moment to introduce him to my plan: to come to me when I summoned him, spend a few intimate hours with me, and immediately leave when the fireworks stopped flying. I did not allow any man to spend the night in my bed. There were three rules to the teddy bear arrangement: no expectations, no questions asked, and no demonstrations of jealousy. I thought it was the perfect arrangement. The key, however, was that I had to be in total control of the situation because my first priority was to my young children—I did not want them to see a strange man in my home for an extended visit. Nowadays, that arrangement is generally initiated by the male and affectionately known as the booty call.

At the end of summer, the radio station hosted a large media event at a downtown hotel for several music celebrities. I was beside myself with excitement to get all dressed up, walk into the hotel, hobnob with the rich and famous, and do a little flirting. I wore a provocative white lace pantsuit and placed a white gardenia in my hair. I looked fabulous, if I must say so myself! I left home in plenty of time to make it to the party on time, but when I got in my car and turned the key, it wouldn't start. The car was fairly new, and the battery was not dead because the lights and radio worked. The engine just wouldn't turn over. I thought to myself, *How strange.* I tinkered under the hood for over an hour trying to make my car start, being careful not to get engine grease on my pretty white outfit. Before finally giving up on going to the party, I turned the key one last time, and the car started. Then I went back into my house and washed my hands before making my way downtown for the party. (Little did I know that God's hand of protection to stop me from going out that night was the reason my car wouldn't start.)

When I arrived at the party, there were lots of well-dressed people there; and the room was full of laughter, cigarette smoke, and loud music. The first person to greet me was RJ. He jokingly said, "Wow, you clean up nicely!" He also told me I was the prettiest thing in the room, and he couldn't keep his eyes or his hands off me. Whenever he touched my arm or pulled me close to him, it felt nice, and I was beginning to entertain thoughts of getting closer to him. The next second, he stepped away to greet some colleagues, so I walked over to the buffet table to help myself sample the food. As I was eating my hors d'oeuvres, RJ came up behind me, kissed me on the neck, and asked me to come with him. When I asked where we were going, he said he wanted to show me some unique artwork upstairs. So I put my plate down and followed him. *There goes dummy again!*

While riding the elevator up to penthouse floor, RJ pulled me close to him, kissed me gently on the lips, and told me I was intoxicating. I pulled back and blushed. When we reached the penthouse, RJ opened the door. I stood in the hallway, strangely looking at him beckoning me to come inside. As I walked through the door of that fabulous hotel room, my instincts overrode my naïveté, and I knew RJ was up to something because I had a bad feeling in the pit of my stomach; so I started backing up toward the door to get out of there.

RJ grabbed my hand and gently pulled me out of the foyer toward the inside of the suite. When I asked him where the art was that he wanted to show me, he said, "It's in the other room." At that instant, I knew he was lying. There was no art. It was a ruse to get me up to that suite. The next thing I knew, RJ was pulling me toward the bedroom parlor. I started pulling back. RJ kept telling me that he knew I wanted him, and he was gonna grant my wish. I broke loose from his tight grip on my wrist and ran out of the bedroom, heading straight for the door. But before I could turn the knob, he wrapped his arms around my belly, lifted me up off the floor, pushed the door close with his foot, and dragged me back to the bedroom. Strength rose from deep inside me, and that night, I put up the fight of my life in that hotel room against RJ.

He chased me from room to room in that hotel suite, tearing off the top of my lace pantsuit and throwing me down on the bed. RJ was strong, but animal instinct infused me with supernatural strength; and he had difficulty overpowering me. Flashbacks from when Marco raped me came rushing into my head. I felt extraordinarily energized as I struggled with RJ. Sheer determination to never again let another man take my body against my wishes made me fight harder. It suddenly became insignificant that I was attracted to RJ or that we had crazy chemistry for each other. Even though I eventually would have responded to his overtures and given in to him, that night, he was not going to forcefully seduce me!

While RJ had me pinned down on the bed, he ripped off the pants to my outfit along with my panty hose, and tried forcing my legs open while lying on top of me. Each time he tried prying my legs apart, I'd clamp them together tightly in a scissor hold. I felt undefeatable! Time and time again, I managed to push RJ off me and jump off the bed only to have him come at me again and throw me back down. During one of the times I struggled with RJ, the hairpiece I was wearing had landed on the floor along with the smashed gardenia from my hair. I was now down to my bra and panties, and determined RJ was not going to overpower me and rape me. We tussled for over an hour as RJ tried to wear me down. Perhaps RJ thought I would tire and simply give in to him, but I never did. I remember saying a quick prayer asking God to help me. Finally, RJ gave up and let me go. I quickly gathered my things, put on my torn clothes, picked up my hairpiece off the floor, clamped it back on my head sideways, and staggered out of that hotel suite. I was exhausted but pleased with myself that I survived an unpleasant ordeal. I discreetly slipped out the back entrance of the hotel, trying not to be seen because I was disheveled and didn't want to explain to anyone why I looked the way I did. But my manager spotted me wobbling along in torn clothes, messed up hair, and a broken high heel and asked, "Vee, are you okay? What happened to you?"

I looked at him, smiled faintly, and answered, "I'm okay. Just a little tired, so don't worry about me. I'll see you Monday!"

That all happened on a Friday night. I figured by the time Monday came when I'd have to go to work, I would have recovered from my ordeal, and my manager might have forgotten about the way I looked. But when Monday came, there were ugly blue bruises up and down both my arms from where RJ had repeatedly grabbed and pinned me down on the bed. I wore a jacket to work so no one would ask me any questions about the bruises. I also neatly folded my torn white outfit that RJ had destroyed and placed it in a shoebox. I put the shoebox in RJ's mailbox at the radio station. Since all the disc jockeys' mailboxes were in my office, I knew I would see RJ that Monday when he came to get his mail.

Sure enough, RJ arrived at the station around noon to dub some commercials. As he passed my office door, he flashed his killer smile and winked at me. I was shocked at his gestures and couldn't believe he felt the need to be smug instead of apologizing for what he had put me through. When he finished making his commercials, he came into my office to get his mail. Seeing the shoebox in his mailbox, he mumbled, "Gee, what's this?"

I got up from my desk, stood very close to him, and whispered in his ear, "That, my friend, is my outfit you ruined Friday night while chasing me around that hotel room trying to get my goodies. And, lover boy, I want the $29.95 that I paid for my pantsuit!" Next I took off my jacket and showed him the bruises he made on my arms when he manhandled me.

To my surprise, RJ became belligerent and told me he wasn't giving me a blankety-blank dime. I looked him straight in his eyes, smiled demurely, and said, "My good man, it's your choice—you can pay me now, or you can pay me later. But rest assured, you *will* pay me." I was careful not to let him see the anger stirring inside of me. All I could think about was how I was going to get back at him for what he had done to me. I wasn't exactly sure whether I'd punish him emotionally or materially. Part of me wanted my plan to be strategic and one that would cost him much more than the $29.95 I was asking for. Another part of me wanted to hurt him emotionally. As the day progressed, I thought about throwing acid on the hood of his car. The way I figured, if he had insurance, the deductible would be more than what I had asked for my pantsuit; and if he didn't have insurance, repairing the hood of his car would really cost him a bundle. By the time my shift ended, I had decided against damaging his property because I wouldn't want anyone to do that to me, so I decided I'd find a way to hurt him on a deeper level—through his emotions.

In case you're wondering why I didn't call the police and report RJ for attempted rape, I can only say that I didn't want to punish him that way. I had other plans for him in my head. He would soon come to clearly understand the old adage: "Hell hath no fury like a woman scorned."

17

Like Father, Like Daughter

Adults find pleasure in deceiving a child. They consider it necessary, but they also enjoy it. The children very quickly figure it out and then practice deception themselves.

—Elias Canetti (1905-1994)

Even though I was a grown woman with two children at this point of my life, I found myself searching my mind for any childhood memory that could explain why I wanted to exact revenge on RJ for what he had done to me instead of reporting him to the authorities for attempted rape.

I remembered a lot of good things I learned from my Dad while growing up, but there were also some not-so-good truths that I remembered about him from which I couldn't escape. My Dad was a seasoned whoremonger and also considered a *player* by today's standard. And because I saw, firsthand, some of his escapades, it was inevitable that I would likely become as masterful a character as he was. During the summers when I was eight and nine years old, Dad would take me with him on Saturdays. He would drive around to local grocery stores and pick up women while I sat in the backseat playing with my dolls. He offered a taxi service to take the ladies home with their groceries. It was called hacking and was a service he only offered to women. Dad was quite a charmer; he was tall, well spoken, and his ruddy skin and red hair really impressed most of the ladies. Many times, he would pick up different women and help them take their groceries into their houses. Sometimes it would be a while before he would return to the car to check on me. Back then, it was commonplace and much safer than it is today for kids to wait in the car while adults ran quick errands. Kids knew to stay put, obey the instructions to not get out of the car, and not touch any knobs or buttons while waiting for the parent to return. I remember times when Dad got back in his car after dropping off a lady hack, he often smelled of cheap perfume. I guess Dad always took me with him because I was loyal; I never told Mom his secrets when she'd question me. Each time I'd get back home after being out with Dad on a Saturday, she'd ask me, "What did you and your Daddy do today?"

My answers were always the same, "Oh, we just rode around town while I played with my doll babies in the backseat of the car."

And Mom always replied, "Vee, I know better. You're just cloaking for your Dad!"

Even though I was just a kid, somehow, I knew there was something wrong with what Dad was doing. I guess that's what Mom meant to accuse me of *cloaking*. However, in looking back at those times, I realize I subconsciously learned about love, lust, and lies from all the observations I made watching my Dad in operation with those ladies. I was his baby girl whom he unknowingly taught many subliminal lessons on deception; consequently, my adult *adventures* were a lot more colorful and destructive than his.

As for my issue with RJ, I decided to mete out a simple but emotionally stinging punishment for him after carefully considering all my options. When I arrived at work Monday morning, following RJ's belligerent reaction to my reimbursement request for the outfit he ruined, I noticed he hadn't taken the shoebox from his mailbox. I discreetly removed it and put it in my desk drawer. That afternoon, RJ came into my office to pick up his mail and noticed the shoebox was gone. He turned to me and gave me a blank stare but said nothing. I smiled back at him, winked, and gave him a very upbeat morning greeting, then immediately shifted my attention back to the work on my desk. No doubt, RJ expected me to still be angry with him, but my perky hello and warm smile confused him. I could see, out of the side of my eye, his mental wheels turning in wonderment.

Over the next few weeks, I continued being playfully seductive with RJ to lull him into a false sense of security that we were, once again, cool with each other. After spewing my charms onto RJ, he began feeling comfortable with me again and quickly resumed making overtures toward me, but I strategically dodged all his advances. Despite the incident in that hotel room the month before, there was no denying there still was crazy chemistry between RJ and me; but I was determined to make him pay an emotional price for what he did to me, and I intended to be the one who called the shots in our *arrangement* per se. Each time RJ propositioned me to go out with him, I would sweetly say, "Perhaps next time, lover boy." Before long, he was begging me to let him take me out to dinner to make up for our *misunderstanding*, as he put it. But I continued to put him off. My plan was to create a passionate curiosity in RJ about me while continuing to reject him until *I was ready to reel him for the kill*. I did that dance with RJ for several months, and just before Thanksgiving, I decided he was ripe for the plucking.

The next time RJ asked me out to dinner, I accepted. He said we could go to any restaurant I wanted, so I chose an upscale place downtown called the 13th Floor. I arranged for my sister to keep my children for the night. I meticulously planned my every move; from the black outfit I wore right down to the fragrance I put on. RJ picked me up from my apartment at 7:30 PM on a Friday night. I made sure I was dressed to the nines to mesmerize him when I opened my front door. When RJ saw me, he let out a moan and told me how spectacular I looked. I had never seen RJ in a suit, so I was quite impressed at how good he looked standing there in my doorway. We arrived at the restaurant just in time for our eight o'clock reservation. Although I picked over my steak, I did eat my lobster tail and dessert. Dinner was good.

As piano music played softly from across the room, RJ asked me if I would dance with him. He said he couldn't wait to hold me close to him, and neither could I! As we glided around the dance floor, I pressed myself against his muscular body and gently ran my hand over his suit jacket, stroking his back. Then I brushed my cheek against his and gently nibbled and tugged on his earlobe with my lips. RJ quietly moaned again and whispered in my ear that he was crazy mad about me. I knew he was burning up with desire, and that pleased me. RJ went on to say how impressed he was over the way I had handled our little *episode* earlier that summer and asked if we could start over. To which I said (while never missing a step), "Why certainly, you can be my teddy bear! As such, our mutual arrangement will be *no questions, no lies, and no expectations*." RJ stopped dancing, stood back, and looked at me with a quizzical look on his face. I'm sure he wasn't expecting me to give him such a direct and well-defined response.

Then pulling me back into an embrace, he said, "Okay, if that's the way you want it."

RJ drove me home and kept squeezing and stroking my hand with an undeniable come-hither look in his eye. I suspected he had an agenda for us but never expected that he would actually be *my* prey. When we arrived back at my apartment, I invited him in for a nightcap. We had just stepped inside of my door when he grabbed me and planted a passionate kiss on my mouth. I knew what was next; but this time, I was armed and ready to take him down. So I initiated some smooth moves that compelled him to undress us both. Our clothes were strewn from my front door to the bedroom. I took his hand, led him over to my bed, and pushed him down hard onto the soft covers. I went into action and intensely made love to him, trying my best to spatter him onto the proverbial headboard. For me, this night was not about pleasure—it was about revenge, and my intent was to cripple RJ with all the unbridled passion I could throw his way. Promiscuity had become an art form for me, so I was well qualified to flex my sexual muscles; and my behavior was likened to that of a lawn mower, and RJ was grass.

Now I admit that the seduction of RJ was magical, and I wasn't disappointed one bit with his sexual prowess, but my *make believe* insatiability that night was hard for him to keep up with because I was on a mission. RJ wasn't dealing with just a woman—that night he had a machine on his hands and I was completely devoid of emotions. It was apparent to me that his reputation of being a good lover had preceded him, so I nicknamed him the Master. Up until that time, he was the best among the other playmates I had had in the past. Our romp lasted two and a half hours, and I tried my best to physically annihilate him. I knew when I finished with RJ that night; he would be so addicted to me that he would be putty in my hands. My moment of triumph came when RJ told me he had never met a woman like me. Then he crawled under the covers with the intention of taking a nap to regain his strength, but I pulled the covers off him and coldly said, "You can go now."

RJ pleaded with me to let him rest for a while, but I told him his work was finished and he had to leave. I reminded him that as my teddy bear, he was not allowed to spend the night in my bed. So he slowly pulled himself up, gathered his clothes from all over the floor, and put them back on. I pulled a cover off my bed and draped myself with it so I could walk him to the door. I gave him a warm hug, gently stroked his groin, and said, "Good job, lover boy. It's been fun!" After RJ left, I leaned against my front door for a brief second or two feeling like Sheena, the Queen of the Jungle, after a mighty kill!

That next week at work was quite interesting, to say the least. When RJ came to my office to pick up his mail, he looked at me all gooey eyed and muttered something about me being an enigma. I reminded him of the rules of our arrangement and told him he wasn't allowed to get all mushy over me because (1) he had a wife, and (2) for me, he was purely just something to do. I went on to reiterate the fact that I knew he was a player just like I was. As such, I was a rolling stone who didn't gather any moss and who didn't want to be tied down. I shared with RJ that I had given him high marks after our date, which put him in the elite category as one of my lovers. The look he gave me was a cross between upset and confusion. I wasn't exactly sure what I would do with RJ in terms of him wanting an exclusive arrangement with me, but when I did make time for us to get together, we didn't waste it going out to dinner; ours was purely a "lust fest" in the pure sense of the word.

Later that day, we had a staff meeting, and I was given the assignment of finding our company another group insurance plan because management wanted to change the one that was in place. I've always been very resourceful even when I have very little information to work with. So I made a few calls and found a Prudential Insurance agent who agreed to come to the station and discuss group insurance options with me. I set the meeting up for the next day. The agent arrived on time and literally bopped when he walked into my office, kinda like an *old* jitterbug. He was a short light-skinned man who oozed with a strange charisma. He introduced himself as Art; and I, in turn, introduced myself as Vee. He pulled out a lot of material and began telling me about various plans that he could set the company up with. As he was giving his pitch, I kept staring at him in a trance-like manner. When he realized I wasn't listening to a thing he was saying, he said, "Ms. Vee, are you okay?"

To which I brazenly replied, "Don't you know lust when you see it?"

Art was obviously startled by my comment, but he remained calm and collected. Then we both laughed, and he proceeded to finish the discussion about insurance.

He gave me his business card and said he'd be back in touch with an insurance quote on the plan I had selected. Just before Art left my office, I shocked him again when I told him I'd like to *borrow him* for about fifteen minutes. I felt like a real hussy that day!

18

And Baby Makes Three

Where did you come from, baby dear?
Out of the everywhere into the here.

—George MacDonald (1824-1905)

The following week, Art returned with the needed insurance information for the radio station to sign the deal for new group coverage. As he was leaving my office, he handed me another business card with his home phone number written on the back. Just as I was taking the card from him, RJ walked into my office to get his mail and heard Art say to me, "Call me. I'm usually home by seven." Art left, and I tucked the card into my pocket. The look on RJ's face was one I'd never seen before. However, once he started to speak, I knew exactly what the look meant. He was jealous!

RJ tried to question me about what was going on between the insurance man and me; but I immediately interrupted him and said, "Wait a second. You have no right to ask me about my social life outside of you. Have you forgotten the rules of our arrangement?" Then I repeated them for him, "*No questions, no lies, no expectations!*" Even though RJ was eleven years older than me, I did not back down from his confrontation. Perhaps he thought since I was much younger than he was, I would cower if he challenged me.

Clearly, RJ was not pleased that I was getting a hookup with another man right in front of him. Once I saw that display of jealously from RJ, I felt empowered to have my hook in him. Having him arrested for our hotel episode paled in comparison to the emotional havoc I knew I could wreak on him. And from the way things were looking, my plan to dominate his thoughts and keep his loins stirred up was working beautifully. As women, we're taught that men are strong and unemotional beings. But I learned from my Dad's behavior that a woman can rock a man to his core; and if she's masterful enough with her words and *wares*, so to speak, she can emotionally manipulate him through his loins. But that kind of addiction can be deadly if mishandled. Remember the movie *Carmen Jones*? She messed up Joe's mind so bad that his jealousy made him kill her so no other man could have her. However, my plan for RJ was not to be a Carmen Jones but to use milder feminine charms on him. Then, after a season of fun with him, pull away and settle into a less intense friendship. RJ seemed to calm down after we talked for a while.

The second week in May, which was a week after Art gave me his card, he called; and asked me to meet him for a drink. After work, we met at his friend's bar in the city. I ordered a soda because I didn't drink, and Art laughed at me for ordering the soda with a cherry in it. He proceeded to drink enough for the both of us. During our conversation, I noticed that we definitely didn't have the chemistry that RJ and I had nor did I feel the ease with Art that I had with RJ when we talked. Art was a much older man, eighteen years my senior to be exact. But I didn't let his age douse my curiosities about him. We hung out at the bar for a few hours; I had several more sodas, and Art had a few more drinks. As I got ready to leave, he said he wanted to show me where he lived and asked me to follow him home. I jokingly commented that it was a good night for me to get my *fifteen minutes* from him.

We arrived at his house a little before 9:00 PM. He poured himself another drink and sat on his couch. Although Art was forty-three years old, shorter than I preferred my men to be, and light skinned, there was a compelling charisma about him that minimized those personal negatives. I decided to cut the night short because I had to get up early for work the next morning. However, before leaving, I quickly switched gears and morphed into my vamp personality. I straddled Art's legs as he was seated on the couch and sat on his lap. Then I announced I was going to *borrow* his little body for about fifteen minutes. He had a little buzz going on, so he didn't resist my advances. It took only six minutes to consummate our union. When I finished, I stood to my feet, straightened myself up, kissed him good night, and left him lying on his couch looking dazed.

Over the next month, we talked a lot by phone and had dinner together once. Because he was an older man, our brief episodes were few and far between, and our rendezvous were always at my apartment. I realized I was *late* the next month despite our sporadic dates, so I immediately stopped taking my birth control pills because I didn't want to chance harming the fetus in case there was one. The last thing I expected was to get pregnant again, especially by a man old enough to be my Dad!

I owned a green 1971 Nova, which Art would borrow from time to time when he had to drive to DC to meet clients because his vehicle needed some repairs and wasn't reliable for traveling long distances. I also helped out with his insurance business by typing letters for him, filling out applications, and the like. Needless to say, Art consumed a lot of my time during the three and a half months we dated, and RJ was not pleased with me that I didn't spend any time with him. However, my focus was on the *situation* I thought I was in.

On Friday, July 20, Dee picked up Pamela and Little Pais because she wanted to take them to the circus that Saturday morning. Since I had my apartment all to myself that night, I invited Art over for us to hang out but primarily to tell him about my missed period. I prepared a nice dinner and listened to him tell me about several deals he was working on. He asked if he could spend the night because he was too tired to drive home, to which I agreed since my children were not there. We went to bed near midnight. I still had not told Art about my missed period, so when he made advances to me for us to be intimate, I didn't put him off because I figured the damage had already been done. I clearly remember that night like it was yesterday. We both *saw stars together*—if you know what I mean. Turns out, July 20 was the night I *actually* got pregnant and not in May when I first seduced Art. I didn't discover that elusive fact until six weeks later.

Art got up early Saturday morning because he had a client appointment while I lay in bed watching him get dressed. I had some time to kill because I didn't have to pick up my children from my sister's house until later that afternoon. As Art was getting dressed, I very calmly told him that I suspected I was pregnant. He stopped tying his tie, sat down on the edge of my bed, and said, "I thought you were on the pill."

I said, "I was, but when I missed my period, I stopped taking them for fear of damaging my baby." Art stood up and slowly finished tying his tie.

As he took his sport coat off the chair where he placed it the night before, he said some cutting words to me, "You can't have this child. You've already got two children! Do you realize the scandal you will face by bringing a bastard into this world?" When he used the word bastard, I cringed.

Immediately, I hopped out of bed, walked over to him, and sternly said, "I'm having this child, and it isn't a bastard. It's *my* baby, so just *go* and forget that you ever met me!" I added that since the pregnancy was not planned but an oops, he should just walk away and act like we never met because this would be my responsibility. After all, I was the one who pursued him. I also told him I wouldn't hold him responsible for anything and that I could take care of myself. Art adamantly kept insisting that I have an abortion—for my *own good* as he put it. He said he didn't want any more kids because he already had two with his wife. And I steadfastly kept saying an emphatic no! Our verbal battle lasted over an hour.

Finally, Art said, "Okay, if you're serious about going through with this pregnancy, I won't leave you holding the bag. I'll help out as much as I can."

I wasn't in love with Art or anything like that, so I didn't interpret his words to mean that because we were having a child, we would be together. God knows I didn't want that. My final words to Art were, "If you're saying you will not walk away from this situation as I've asked you to but are saying you will help with some of the expenses for the child, I *will* hold you to your word. So be *very* careful to say what you mean, and mean what you say. Since you've given me your word, I hope you won't renege."

Art left that Saturday morning, and I didn't hear from him for three months. It wasn't a problem for me that I didn't speak with him for such a long time because I didn't need anything from him at that point nor was there anything I needed to say to him. Simply put, he was merely a flash in the pan. However, I did plan to contact him when I gave birth to let him know if he had a son or a daughter and to ask him to buy the baby a crib. I truly believed when I missed my period I had gotten pregnant in May (after forgetting to take my birth control pills a couple days that month). Imagine my surprise when I learned that I didn't actually conceive until the night of July 20. In any event, it was not a guess anymore because my doctor visit in September confirmed my pregnancy. Since I was still legally married to Sack and covered under his family insurance plan at work, I had no worries about my medical bills.

After getting the official word that I was, in fact, pregnant again, I went to see my Dad. We had become very close since I had my children. He was especially proud of Little Paisley, his only grandson whom I had named after him. Whenever I couldn't pay my phone or utility bill and would get a turnoff notice, I went to Dad for his help, and he would pay them for me. He would also reprimand me for waiting until my money problems became a crisis situation before coming to him for help. I basically believed I could work things out to pay them myself, but before I knew it, due dates would come and go.

I went to see my Dad that day so I could tell him I was having another baby and share my plans with him on how I intended to exile myself from everyone and move far away into Randallstown to minimize the ridicule I would face. I told him the hospital bill for the baby's delivery would be covered by insurance; but in the meantime, before I gave birth, I would have a small hardship situation buying gas for my car to drive back and forth to work from Randallstown. My Dad looked up from his dinner plate and said, "Vee, mistakes happen. Just don't stay down when you fall. This child will not want for anything as long as I am alive. And to help out, I will give you $10 a week." I thanked my Dad, kissed his cheek, and went upstairs to visit with my mother. I knew her reaction to my baby news would not be good, but I bit the bullet and told her anyway. My mother called me a whore and told me I needed to be with my husband because he still loved me. She added that a half a loaf of bread is better than no loaf at all.

Out of respect, I didn't argue with my mother but smiled at her and said, "Ma, man shall not live by bread alone." At that point, she stopped talking to me about Sack and changed the subject. After visiting an hour or so, I left and went home.

By the end of the next month, I had moved out of my apartment and into a larger apartment far into a rural community in Randallstown. My Dad did as he promised and faithfully gave me $10 each Sunday to cover the extra expense I had driving back and forth to work since I lived quite a long way from the city.

My job at the radio station came to an abrupt end when I discovered a hidden bookkeeping error in a commission underpayment to one of the salesmen. I brought the $952 error to Diamond Jim's attention. He, in turn, confronted the station manager about the discrepancy in his commission check since the manager was the one who calculated the sales commissions and wrote the checks. Little did I know I had uncovered an iceberg of embezzlement that was well hidden by the station manager and was not supposed to be discovered by anyone, let alone an unsuspecting secretary!

That following week, a day before payday, I was called to the station manager's office. I wasn't "showing" yet, so I had no concerns over the discussion being about my pregnancy. The manager told me to have a seat and proceeded to tell me that the station was having financial difficulties and needed to cut costs in a few places—and one of those places was in salaries. Then he announced they could no longer afford to pay my $250-a-week salary and would be reducing my pay by 50 percent. If I wanted to keep my job, I should accept the 50 percent pay cut. My gut sensed he was not telling me the truth, but I couldn't hone in on what the real truth was to challenge him. I was too stunned to question him, and my shock showed on my face. I got up from my seat and told him I would think about his offer and let him know my decision the next day.

Thoughts raced through my head as I walked back to my office. *If I stayed, how could I live on $125 a week? How could I pay my rent, car payment, and day care for the kids on half of what I had been earning? Soon there would be another mouth to feed in six more months. How was I going to manage that? Should I accept the offer and get myself a part-time job or what?* As I did the math, it was apparent to me I had to turn down the station offer and look for another job. This was definitely a searing *Oh! Jesus* moment. Instead of feeling sorry for myself about the upsetting situation that was facing me, I drew on my faith and took a minute to pray. I admitted to God that I was in a situation I didn't know what to do about, but I trusted Him completely to help me get through it. I asked for his help and thanked him for taking care of me.

The next morning, Diamond Jim came into my office and closed the door behind him. He thanked me for finding the error in his commission payments and confidentially shared a conversation with me he overheard the day before. Diamond Jim confirmed my suspicion that there was no financial difficulty at the station, but a move to get me out of the company. The plan was to ask me to do the same job for half the pay so I would quit. Apparently, I was too smart for my own good having discovered that deliberate shortage of a commission payment due to the top salesman. My suspicions of embezzlement were confirmed. No doubt, other salesmen had also been cheated out of some of their commission payments, and the station manager wanted me out of there before I discovered his scheme and exposed him. Diamond Jim swore me to secrecy and told me he would deny everything he told me if I went back to the station manager with the information he shared with me. I promised him I wouldn't say a word to anybody. God was clearly working in my behalf to let me learn that truth. The next thing that happened astonished me.

I was typing rapidly on my typewriter when a dapper little guy walked down the office hallway, making a clickety-clackety sound with his shoes, came into my office. He was dressed in a leather suit, cowboy boots with cleats, and a leather cowboy hat. He stopped dead in his steps and said, "Great googamooga, girl, it sounds like a Teletype machine in here!"

I looked up from my typewriter to see a short but handsome bald-headed caramel-colored man standing in the doorway looking at me strangely. He had a Charlie Chan mustache and a well-trimmed goatee. His hands were nicely manicured, and he was quite articulate when he spoke. His flawless skin captured my attention. He lowered his pipe and kindly explained that he was also a disc jockey and had come to our station to buy airtime for a stage show he was promoting. He introduced himself to me as *The Commander*, but said his real name was Maurice Hulbert.

He walked over to my desk, leaned in close, and very softly asked me if I would be interested in working for him because he needed someone who typed well to work in his home office. My rapid typing really impressed him. I couldn't believe my ears! God had literally sent this man right to my door with a job offer! I stood up from my chair, introduced myself, and whispered, "As a matter of fact, Mr. Hulbert, I just so happen to be in the market for another job." Then I told him about my job ending that very day and confidentially told him I was in a family way. He said my pregnancy wasn't a problem for him if it wasn't a problem for me. He offered to pay me $225 a week and asked how soon I could start because he was in dire need of a secretary. He clearly spelled out his expectations and quickly described the duties of the job. They were pretty basic to me—answer the phone, balance his checkbook, and type letters, contracts, and memos. I graciously accepted his offer on the spot, shook his hand, and told him he had just hired himself a new secretary. He smiled at me and said, "VOSA!" Needless to say, I did a quick sprint to the station manager's office and informed him I could not accept his offer and would be gone by the end of that day.

I started working for Mr. Hulbert that following Monday. Not only was there no break in my income but because I was paid in cash, I actually had more take-home pay.

19

She Works Hard for the Money

*Hard work spotlights the character of people: some turn up their sleeves,
Some turn up their noses, and some don't turn up at all.*

—Sam Ewing (1921-)

Working for Mr. Hulbert was a very pleasant experience. He was the epitome of professionalism in everything he did, and I learned a lot from him. He was a famous radio personality who was the first full-time black DJ on an all-white radio station when he was hired at WITH in Baltimore. He was also a promoter of talent shows and beauty pageants. However, when I worked for him, his radio career primarily was spent in sales and show promotions and not as much on-air time.

He resided in a swank two-bedroom apartment in the city, and his office was set up in the second bedroom. He regularly commuted to Philadelphia to his primary home with his wife and children. When I began working for him, the office was a bit of a mess with piles of papers everywhere, but I assured Mr. Hulbert that I'd have it organized and standing tall in no time. I was thrilled that he had an electric typewriter for me to use instead of a manual one. But either way, I was just happy to have that job.

I didn't have any reservations about working alone with Mr. Hulbert in his apartment because he was always a gentleman and very respectful to me. At that time, he was fifty-six years old, and I had a lot of respect for the man. On the surface, it probably didn't look good for a young woman half his age to go into that apartment every morning and leave every evening. Despite how it looked; *The Commander* was a master at what he did for a living, and I really didn't care about *appearances* but was simply excited about learning new things in the entertainment industry. Answering his busy phone afforded me many opportunities to speak with celebrities. It seemed like everyone knew Mr. Hulbert, but everyone mostly referred to him as Rod because of his stage name, Hot Rod. His famous on-air quote was "Not the flower, not the herb, not the root, but the seed. VOSA," which meant *voice of sound advice*! Another "Roddism" was the greeting he first gave to me—great googamooga!

One day, I answered his phone, and it was Lou Rawls on the other end of the line; I almost fainted! It was really *him*, and there was no mistaking that deep, cool voice when he asked to speak with *The Commander*. Another time, I took a call from Louis Gossett Jr. (whom I later met and still cherish the picture taken of us together.)

As the months rolled by, my tummy grew bigger and bigger. It became more and more uncomfortable for me to sit all day, especially with the baby kicking me most of the time. In my sixth month of the pregnancy, I learned to type standing up! Mr. Hulbert was very pleased with my work and often told me so. Sometimes, he would come into the office to talk to me, sit on the couch in there, rub his bald head, and go on and on about how organized I was and how much he appreciated all the hard work I did to get and keep him straight. At first, he micromanaged me until he found out I would get all my work done and not goof off. I was a loyal employee and did not take advantage of his trust. He valued me more than any other boss I ever worked for. Making his life less chaotic was my primary objective, and I quickly became known as Rod's Girl Friday.

One day in late fall, my Dad called me at work and asked me to accompany him to a doctor appointment at the University of Maryland the next week. He said he had been hoarse for a long time and wanted to get it checked out. Of course I said yes, even before clearing the time off with Mr. Hulbert. I told my boss about the appointment, and he gladly agreed to me taking the time off to go with my Dad to the doctor. The only downside of working for Mr. Hulbert was I did not earn leave like I would have had I worked for a traditional employer, so that meant I wouldn't get paid for any time I took off. However, that particular time, Mr. Hulbert didn't dock my pay for the four hours I was out of the office with my Dad at the hospital. I was really grateful for his generosity.

After Dad saw the doctor, I went into the doctor's office to speak privately with him about Dad's hoarseness not getting any better. What he told me was heart wrenching. The doctor said my Dad had lung cancer. I asked if it was terminal, and he said yes and recommended that Dad take radium and cobalt treatments, which could sustain him for another year or so. Since his cancer was too far gone to cure, the treatments would basically give him more quality time. The doctor explained that the radiation would cause a large purple mark on Dad's back, which we could use as a gauge. As his body used the radium to fight the cancer, the purple mark would get smaller and smaller. When the mark completely disappeared, Dad's time would be minimal.

My Dad was sixty-eight years old when he was diagnosed with lung cancer. I had three months left before I was to give birth, and I so desperately wanted my father to see his third grandchild. At that time, medical science was very limited in the field of cancer treatments, and expecting a cure for his lung cancer was unrealistic since it wasn't caught in its early stage. There was no answer to the question of how long it would be before my Dad died. All I knew was I had to bring him as much joy and comfort I could for the time he had left. The following week, Dad began his radiation treatments. His cough and hoarseness seemed to improve but did not completely disappear. After he completed his first round of radiation, he seemed like himself again.

When February came, it grew increasingly harder each day for me to get up mornings and wobble into work. Although Mr. Hulbert was very accommodating to me, making sure my chair was comfortable and insisting that I take lots of breaks to stretch my legs and back, there were still many days where nothing seemed to help the discomfort of carrying my baby. As big as I was, I thought my baby would be a nine pounder!

Because Pamela and Little Paisley's birthdays were approaching soon, I had to get busy putting a party together for them. Pamela was turning a big five years old on February 11, and Little Pais was turning three on February 12. Since their birthdays were back-to-back, it was easier for me to give them a joint party. Amazingly, I mustered up the energy to shop for pink and blue invitations, plan kiddie activities for fifteen kids, order one blue cake and one pink cake, and clean up my apartment for their big day. The party started at 2:00 PM, Saturday, February 12, without a hitch. There were fifteen rambunctious kids ripping and running through my apartment for three hours, and my sister was a tremendous help (and lifesaver) to me that day. Needless to say, everyone had a good time, and I was beyond tired when the day was over! Both of my children were so very happy with all their neat birthday gifts.

When that first weekend in March rolled around, I was so weary from being pregnant that I got the bright idea that I could speed up my delivery by swallowing a tablespoon of castor oil. (I had heard several of my aunts talk about how a woman shouldn't take castor oil late in her pregnancy because that will bring on labor pains.) So I poured myself a tablespoon of the stuff, gagged trying to get it down, and waited on Mother Nature to do her thing. In about four hours, my stomach began to hurt, and full-blown contractions began. I thought I would be dropping my load sooner rather than later, so I called my doctor when my contractions were five minutes apart. (I had used the same obstetrician for Pamela and Little Pais's birth.) Dr. Radmann told me to go right to the hospital, and he would see me there. It was Saturday, and I figured I would have my baby that weekend.

When I arrived at Sinai Hospital that Saturday afternoon, I was crouched over in a lot of pain, holding my stomach. I actually had forgotten that the castor oil was the reason I was having contractions and thought my baby was actually ready to be born! Dr. Radmann came into the examining room and checked me out. After he examined me, much to my chagrin, he said I was just having *false* labor because I was not even dilated. Imagine that! My plan did not work. The next day, I went to visit my Dad. He was in his bedroom, sitting in the recliner that Dee and I had bought him for Father's Day the year before. We talked briefly about how he was feeling, and I shared with him the anxiety I was experiencing with my pregnancy. To me, Dad was a sage whose wisdom I revered, so I asked him if he had any idea when the baby would be born. He got up out of his chair, walked over to a calendar hanging on his wall, turned the page to April, pointed to the thirteenth, and said, "Vee, you will have the baby on the thirteenth of April." And six weeks later, I woke up the morning of April 12 with water seeping slowly out of me. I wasn't sure what was happening to me until my mother told me my water was breaking. When I delivered my other two children, the doctor broke my water once I was on the delivery table, so I never had that experience before.

I called Mr. Hulbert and told him I wouldn't be coming to work because I was in labor and probably would be having my baby that day. My mother told me to start walking to speed up the delivery, but I wanted to wait for my sister's shift to end so she could take me to the hospital since I couldn't drive myself. Then I remembered the story Mom told me about how she slowed up her labor process by "sitting on me all day" while waiting on Dad to get home from work before giving birth. I wasn't sure if there was any validity to that story or whether it was an old wives' tale, but I decided to give it a try.

I did sit in a chair for most of the day; my pains were not really that hard, but I would seep each time I got up from my chair. Around 7:00 PM, I got up from the chair and began walking briskly around my living room. My pains quickly became more intense and closer together. I called my doctor when the pains were five minutes apart—again. This time, it was the real McCoy; I was definitely having my baby. Dee picked me up and got me to the hospital at exactly 11:30 PM. I was prepped quickly; and Dr. Radmann helped me give birth to a beautiful eight-pound, thirteen-ounce blue-eyed little darling at 1:03 AM, April 13—just like Dad said I would. I named him Phillip. (State law prohibited me from listing Art on my baby's birth certificate as his Dad because I was still legally married to Sack. The law required that my husband be listed as the father.)

The next morning, the phone in my room rang, waking me up; it was Mr. Hulbert. He asked me what I had, how was I doing, and when I was coming back to work! I was real groggy but managed to abruptly reply, "Mr. Hulbert, I just had a baby! I'm in no shape to come to work just yet. I'll call you soon." He chuckled and told me to get well but to hurry back because he missed me.

At that time, I didn't know that my mother had contacted Sack to tell him I had had the baby until he came to the hospital the next day after I delivered. He brought me a large bouquet of my favorite flowers, gladiolas, and a box of Whitman's chocolates, just like he always did when we were together. When Sack returned from the nursery after looking at Phillip, to my shock and amazement, he said, "Honey, we have *another* beautiful son!" At that moment, unshakable respect emerged and remains in me for Sack over his love for all my children even though Paisley is his only biological child. We had been separated for three long years, but he said he still loved me and wanted us to be a family. He told me when my mother gave him the news several months ago that I was pregnant, he told her that he still loved me *anyway* and that the child I was carrying was a part of him because it was a part of me. He begged me to come back to him and bring *his* children home. I told Sack I appreciated his kindness to me but explained that we were done, and I wanted him to get on with his life and settle down with someone else who would do right by him. He didn't like what he heard but said he understood. I was surprised and pleased that Sack wasn't agitated and upset with me. As he was leaving, he commented again on what a beautiful baby Phillip was. Three days later, my son and I were released from the hospital to go home. Dee picked us up and took us home.

I was a twenty-six-year-old mother of a five-year-old, a three-year-old, and a three-day-old infant; and the magnitude of that responsibility loomed large in my mind. As the sole support for those three young lives, I vowed to give them the best life I possibly could as long as I breathed God's air. I was also acutely aware of the fact that I *could not* raise my children without God's help. Now it was time to get in touch with my baby's father to let him know he had a son and to ask him to buy a crib for Phillip. I called Art's office that Monday and was told he was in the Bahamas at a sales meeting. When he returned from his trip, I called him repeatedly, but he did not return any of my calls. Anger began to well up inside me toward that man for the heartless disregard he demonstrated by deliberately dodging my calls and not keeping his word to help with the baby's expenses. All I wanted was for him to buy our baby a crib! What Art didn't know about me was I *could not* let him get away with such irresponsibility, especially since he didn't accept my offer to walk away from me when I gave him the *out*. I planned to *go for his jugular*, so to speak, and guarantee that indigestion would well up in his belly at the very mention of my name. Put simply, Art would rue the day he met me when I was finished with him!

My Dad bought my baby a bassinet to sleep in, and my sister showered me with many needed baby items for Phillip's comfort. Pamela was in kindergarten, and Little Pais was in nursery school, so I was able to sleep during the day with my newborn while my other two children were away during the day. However, eighteen days after giving birth to Phillip, I went back to work because I needed my salary to support my growing family.

Mr. Hulbert was gracious enough to allow me to bring my baby, in his bassinet, to work. I fed and changed my son throughout the day in between typing up contracts, answering the phones, and maintaining the office. Phillip was a *good* baby with a very peaceful disposition. He ate, slept a lot, and cried very little. And although my stress level had gone up a notch with a new baby, I was a very blessed mother of three divine little souls.

I have learned that . . .

- Trying hard does not always make you a winner.
- Adversity is not punishment.
- All human situations have their inconveniences.
- A lie told often enough can become one's truth.
- Actions can lie louder than words.
- Passion mishandled is like setting fire to dry straw.

Section IV

The Yellow Road

> **Grace** is not a strange, magic substance
> which is subtly filtered into our souls
> to act as a kind of spiritual penicillin.
> Grace is unity, oneness within ourselves,
> oneness with God.
>
> Thomas Merton (1915-1968)

I made a series of bad choices that put me on a collision course with lunacy. My life was a blueprint of collateral dysfunction. Those choices, and many failures, made me face some really hard truths about myself and admit I needed help. The most courageous thing I've ever done was to *stand still* and allow the wheels of a train called *grace* to slowly roll over me.

20

Don't Get Mad, Get Even

Indeed, it's always a paltry, feeble, tiny mind that takes pleasure in revenge. You can deduce it without further evidence than this that no one delights more in vengeance than a woman.

—Juvenal (c. AD 60-c. 130)

Eventually, I was able to get in touch with Art to tell him about the birth of his son although he quickly denied that it was his child. Part of me completely understood his doubt about Phillip being his child given the less-than-ladylike manner in which I entered his life and seduced him. Nonetheless, his denial of our son did not negate the certainty that he was, in fact, Phillip's Dad.

During that exhaustive phone conversation with Art, I reminded him of the opportunity he was extended to *walk away* from my pregnancy because it was "*my oops*," as the unplanned event that it was. I went on to refresh his memory of his useless attempts to convince me to abort my baby and his retort to *not leave me holding the bag but help with expenses*. We were at an impasse. The rejection I felt on the phone that day was devastating when Art denied his paternity, summarily dismissed me, and hung up. Perhaps it was my naïveté, but I just couldn't believe we were having a disagreement over our child. It was apparent Art was clueless about how tenacious and resourceful I could be. He obviously believed his experience with life would trump my inexperience and make me give up on him accepting responsibility for Phillip. I had a point to prove, and I wasn't backing down. Truth be told, Phillip was the crown jewel of motherhood for me. I didn't know it then; but making the choice to stand up to the scandal I faced, trusting the Lord to help me through my mess, and having my baby were undoubtedly the gateway to all the unimaginable blessings I have received from God.

As early as I can remember from my childhood, *disappointment* has always been a challenge for me—and it still is. When anyone tells me they are going to do something, I expect them to keep their word or at least tell me if things change and they no longer can do what they initially said they would. This is a *simple* principle. So when Art said he would help with expenses, I believed him. But since Art was denying the help he initially offered me because he didn't believe he was my baby's father, we genuinely had ourselves a slight problem.

Clearly, my focus had to take a temporary detour from being a sweet, loving person to being somewhat of a mercenary; I now had to deal with a paternity issue and suspected that it wasn't going to be a cakewalk. I shared with Mr. Hulbert the situation I was going through with Phillip's Dad and told him he would need to replace me in a few months because I needed to find another job with benefits so I could carry the health insurance on my family. Mr. Hulbert completely understood and asked that when I found a job, I would give him as much notice as I possibly could. I agreed.

After realizing Art was not budging, I immediately embarked on a road that I knew very little about, the legal circuitry to file a paternity petition. I quickly managed to gather information and the necessary paperwork I needed for the huge task that was before me. A vindictive side of me surfaced that I didn't know I had until I started moving the ball around for the petition. I was determined to not stop short of getting court-ordered child support and filing an ethics complaint with Art's employer because of the irresponsible behavior he demonstrated after getting me pregnant and rejecting my offer to walk away from me. In other words, I became Art's worst nightmare. The legal process was arduous, time-consuming, and frustrating; but I dug my heels in and pulled out every stop I could to win my case.

When I first applied for child support, Art's attorney returned the paperwork to the social services department with an official denial of paternity, so the court ordered a blood test to settle the dispute between us.

On four separate occasions, Art was a no-show in court before the judge, but I persevered. Growing tired of his antics, I decided to up the ante and paid his employer a visit to lay the groundwork for my ethics complaint. After my lengthy conversation with his boss, Art magically appeared in court for our next hearing. The blood test was done on both of us; and the results were indisputable that Phillip was, in fact, our child. After reaching that milestone, child support was finally granted, and I was awarded $12.50 a week toward Phillip's support. Several months after the paternity case was settled and my meeting with Art's boss, he was demoted from the management position he held. Needless to say, he was incensed with me for all I had done to him. Many months passed without hearing from Art, and the child support payments became sporadic after Art left that large corporation he worked for. However, by the time Phillip entered third grade, he and his Dad had met each other, and their father-son relationship began to grow and flourish. They now have a healthy relationship.

An amazing thing happened to me one Saturday in early September when I went to the bank with my children to cash my paycheck. What I identified as a *blessing from God* was, in truth, an act of dishonesty on my part. While conducting my banking business, I sat my infant's carryall seat on top of the counter with him strapped inside. Phillip was a really, really beautiful baby with sky blue eyes and round and puffy little cheeks that compelled anyone who looked at him to gently squeeze them. Pam and Little Pais stood politely beside me, playing quietly with each other until I was finished my business. Little Pais *also* attracted lots of attention from females with his Dad's dazzling hazel eyes, and that day was no exception. It was a regular occurrence for women to squeeze Paisley's cheeks and put money in his little hands. That day, the bank teller was so attracted to my beautiful children, especially baby Phil's blue eyes and peaceful disposition, that she miscounted my change. As I quickly thumbed through my money, I realized I had an extra $424. I nervously folded the envelope, hurriedly put it inside my diaper bag, dashed out of the bank, hopped into my car, and quickly drove home. I convinced myself that money was heaven-sent! Of course, there was a tiny little voice inside of my head, which I knew was godly conviction, telling me I should have given that money back to the bank teller. But instead, I chose to view the money as an unexpected *miracle* (and silenced that voice with the justification that the bank had more money than I ever would have), kept it, and decided to take my three—and five-year-old children to the new Disney World amusement park that had recently opened in Orlando, Florida. My sister agreed to keep my baby for the four days we would be gone, and I immediately started making plans for the vacation. Next I contacted Sack to let him know the kids and I would be out of town for the weekend so he wouldn't be upset about not seeing them on his scheduled visit.

I called Eastern Air Lines and made reservations for the three of us to fly to Orlando for a brief vacation and see the fun new place that Walt Disney had just opened. At that time, there were only two hotels inside of the park within walking distance to all the attractions. One was an apex-looking structure called the Contemporary and the other was a Tahitian-looking hotel called the Polynesian Village. I chose the Polynesian because it had a beach right outside of its hotel rooms. That extra $424 paid for our airfare, our hotel accommodations, and food. That was the first time my children flew on an airplane, and I *secretly* thanked Equitable Trust Bank for making it happen for them. Pam and Pais enjoyed seeing Mickey Mouse, and Donald Duck, as well as getting on every single ride in each of the parks. My favorite attraction was the Country Bear Jamboree. Needless to say, I was tired from our daily adventures, ripping and running through the various attractions. (Disney World was on a much smaller scale in 1972.) We packed a lot of living into those three nights and four days we were in Orlando, and flying back home was bittersweet. When we arrived at the airport, my children were proudly wearing their Mickey Mouse ears, and everyone they spoke to commented on how cute they looked. To my surprise, Sack, my estranged husband, met us at the gate and took lots of pictures of Pam and Pais in their hats. (He was still hopeful that we would get back together.)

I believe joy comes from embracing the circumstances and seasons of life where God has put you and accepting the responsibilities that come with that season. And the season of my life that I was in then required a lot of me. Since the paternity fiasco was behind me, and I had just enjoyed a mini vacation, it was necessary that I concentrate my energies on finding a better job. Mr. Hulbert was very supportive and wrote me a glowing letter of reference. I regularly combed through the newspaper, searching for another job as well as registering with several employment agencies. By the fall of that year, I had found a wonderful position as an executive secretary with a railroad company located in Washington DC.

21

Charlie, My Charlie

We must accept finite disappointment, but never lose infinite hope.

—Martin Luther King (1929-1968)

Traveling to my new job demanded that my day start early each morning, so I asked my mother to help me out by keeping my boys. She would not agree to keep them, so I had to find a sitter for Phillip and a day care center for my other two children. I was ecstatic when I found a babysitter for my infant son and a nursery school that agreed to keep my three-year-old son and five-year-old daughter. I needed to be at my job by 9:00 AM, so I dropped off my baby at 7:00 AM at the sitter and dropped my other two older children at the nursery school by 7:30 AM. The nursery school took my five-year-old to school each day, picked her up from her half day of kindergarten, and brought her back to the center with her brother. Although my morning and evening day care routine was rigorous, I was able to start my new job with a sense of relief about my children's care since they were safe and well cared for during the day. I discovered that my daily drive to and from Washington was therapeutic because it relaxed me, and I was able to decompress any stress that hit me either in the morning or at the end of my day. However, because DC traffic moved very fast, I taught myself to drive with two feet so I could quickly change lanes in rush hour traffic to keep up with the flow of all the cars.

I was assigned to the real estate department, and the office where I worked was lovely. A brand-new electric typewriter was sitting on the desk awaiting my arrival that first day on the job, and that made me happy. My primary responsibility was typing railroad contracts. I settled into my job and quickly became the most productive secretary in the department because of my proficient and accurate typing. The office building that I worked in was very large, and early on, I got lost often trying to find my way to my office. One day, I was late returning from lunch and mistakenly got off on the wrong floor and walked into the wrong office. I must have had quite a look of astonishment on my face because the fella sitting at the front desk smiled and asked if he could help me. After I realized I was on the wrong floor, I shyly replied that I was lost and had not been paying attention when I got off the elevator.

The gentleman got up from his desk, walked over to me, introduced himself, and offered to show me how to get back to my office. He said his name was Charlie. As we walked back to the elevator, in a soft but seductive voice, he commented how delighted he was that I had accidentally walked into his office. I believed he was hitting on me. Charlie rode with me on the elevator and graciously showed me the way up to my office. Although I was embarrassed, I was intrigued by the way Charlie talked and laughed with me. He was a lighthearted, funny guy with a hypnotic-like sense of humor that made me laugh despite my attempts to stay focused on getting to the right floor. Charlie asked me my name and then disappeared back into the elevator after showing me where to go. Because we worked on separate floors, in different departments, I had never run into Charlie before that fateful encounter. But after we met, I started seeing Charlie up on my floor at least three days a week over the next month. He would walk past my office, throw up his hand, wave, and wink at me. I knew Charlie could sense I liked him by the way I blushed whenever he did his special greeting. Before long, I looked forward to his weekly waves and winks.

One day as I was rushing to go home at the end of my shift, I bumped into Charlie in the hallway as we both were heading toward the front door of the building. We exchanged pleasantries, and then he asked me if I would have lunch with him. I blushed and immediately said yes to his invitation. We agreed to meet the next day. The rest of that evening, I was a nervous mess. I could hardly concentrate on getting my kids fed, bathed, and in bed without constantly thinking about Charlie. When I finally crawled into bed for the night, I was still wound up with excitement, and it took several hours to fall asleep. When morning came, I was very tired and sleepy from a restless night. Anxious anticipation of spending time with Charlie made my adrenaline kick in, and I went about my normal routine seamlessly. I actually arrived at my office fifteen minutes earlier than I normally did because I wanted to make sure there were no assignments in my in-basket that would prevent me from keeping my 12:30 PM lunch appointment with Charlie.

Because the contracts I typed each day were time sensitive, I certainly didn't want one to cross my desk that had to be typed up, processed, and faxed out by 12:30 PM to a West Coast affiliate. I made up my mind that if a West Coast contract request did come through, I fully intended to pawn it off on one of the other secretaries in the typing pool. Fortunately, my lunch hour rolled around without a hitch. Charlie came to my office to pick me up. He had on a very nice tie, which was out of the norm for him, and some drop-dead good-smelling cologne. As he walked over to my desk, the smile on my face spoke volumes. At that instance, I believe anyone looking at me could see all my back teeth from the big smile I was wearing. Needless to say, I felt as if I was walking on a cloud! It was quite obvious to me that Charlie had put a lot of preparation into the way he looked for our first date.

We went to a very nice restaurant on K Street. I ordered a grilled cheese sandwich and a glass of iced tea, and Charlie ordered a juicy hamburger and fries. To my surprise, I was able to finish my sandwich and drink even though this man mesmerized me. We talked about our families, our hobbies, and what we liked to do for fun. I learned that he was a sports aficionado, and he bowled every week on a league. His birthday was March 15, and he was Pisces. I was a natural magnet for Pisces men albeit not an ideal match for me, but nonetheless a uniquely exciting union. Since my three children dominated my life, I didn't have any hobbies to tell him about. But he seemed genuinely interested in hearing about each of my children. Charlie didn't waste any time letting me know he was very fond of me and asked if I would be agreeable to us dating each other, except he wanted it to be exclusive. Then he sprung the news on me that he wanted to take me to his college homecoming weekend in two weeks. I told him that I'd have to think about his proposition and get back to him. He wrote his phone number down on a napkin and told me to put it in a safe place.

Up until that time, I had no experience with a long-distance relationship, let alone an *exclusive* arrangement; so I had to really think long and hard whether I wanted to be tied down in a relationship with one man and especially a coworker! However, because I was very careful not to expose my children to strange men, I only dated casually and did not allow myself to have exclusive relationships. That way, it prevented my kids from asking me a lot of questions if the relationship didn't work out.

As we were walking back to work from our lunch date, Charlie pulled me close to his side and said, "Don't break my heart 'cause I'm crazy 'bout you, girl!" Clearly, a part of me loved that lover-boy persona, but another part of me thought Charlie was a little on the dull side and unable to hold my interest.

That night, I called my sister to talk about my lunch date with Charlie and get her opinion on the situation. My excitement was very hard to contain as I told her about my day. I can always tell my big sis about what's going on in my life and come away from our conversations with a clear sense of the best way in which I should go. I count on her attentively listening to me and throwing in one of her one-liners to make me laugh. When I finished my spiel, she reminded me that because Charlie and I lived over forty-five miles away from each other, she didn't see where there would be a problem with him being *around* too much since I could control his visits to my neck of the woods. More importantly, she suggested I continue to maintain my children's privacy by going to his side of town. I shared with her that he wanted to take me to his college homecoming weekend and needed me to make up my mind about our *relationship* so he could finalize plans if I would be accompanying him as his girlfriend.

I admitted to my sister that my curiosities about Charlie were primarily physical (as usual) and not so-much-so companion driven. Once I heard myself admit that truth, my decision was pretty easy. That next night, I called Charlie at home. We made small talk for about five minutes before he asked me if I had thought any more about our lunch conversation. I told him that I had given our conversation a lot of thought and had decided I would be his girlfriend, but at some point in the very near future, we needed to discuss ground rules.

We kept our relationship very quiet at work because we didn't want to chance getting into trouble for having a workplace romance. In some corporations, that's a no-no, so we behaved civilly to each other around the company officials. However, our close friends knew we were an item by the way we interacted with each other. When I did get to discuss my *ground rules* with Charlie, he was okay with my desire to not bring him around my children and not show up at my house unannounced. Charlie did finally get to meet my kids when I had a party at my apartment later that summer. He was one of the many guests my children met. Charlie was especially taken by Phillip's charm and inquisitive nature. He loved the way Phillip always said "Why" to everything. No doubt, Phillip was his favorite of my three children, and he never failed to always ask me about Little Phil—as he called him—every time we talked.

I went to Charlie's homecoming weekend and had a fabulous time. As we watched the football game in the stadium, I truly enjoyed the one-on-one attention Charlie showered me with. It was a novel experience for me and I tried really hard to settle into it with as much ease as I could muster up. That weekend, my sexual curiosities about Charlie were settled. I was correct; he was quite dull and unassuming, and I quickly discovered that he didn't lie about being a sports fanatic! What he didn't tell me was just how much of a fanatic he was. Specifically, Charlie regularly opted to watch TV sports over *romancing* me. Whenever there was any type of contact sport on TV like baseball, football, or basketball, Charlie did not have time for me and acted like I wasn't even in the room. I regularly played second fiddle to his television set.

Since I did not share his passion for sports, I eventually grew tired of being his afterthought during those times I visited him. When a commercial came on, Charlie would always say something funny to make me laugh, and I would settle down for another couple of hours or so. However, the final straw of our relationship was the time I cooked all his favorite dishes—at his request, no less—and invited him to my house for dinner, only to be stood up for a play-off game. He called me and callously told me to throw out the dinner because he wasn't coming over. He gave no apology.

After enduring eleven months of Charlie's neglect because of his obsession with sports, I ended the silliness in our intimate relationship, such as it was; but we still kept in touch with each other. After our breakup, Charlie ironically became my best friend and often teased me about breaking his heart when I left him. He was always fun to talk with, and I loved how he always made me laugh with his dry sense of humor. Charlie never got married. Over the years, he would always ask how my children were doing and reminded me to let him know if they ever needed anything. Three years in a row, he actually sent me a check to help buy Christmas toys for my children. Charlie was a unique individual with a big heart for helping others when they were in trouble. Our friendship continued for over thirty-five years and over time, he gradually became a recluse.

Charlie passed away suddenly after falling in his shower a week after my 60th birthday. I really miss him, and think of him often.

22

Gone, but Not Forgotten

It matters not how a man dies, but how he lives.
The act of dying is not of importance, it lasts so short a time.

—Samuel Johnson (1709-1784)

Over the next two years, my life ebbed and flowed in unimaginable ways. On the plus side, my job with the railroad was going well, the children were growing nicely, and I had moved into a lovely townhouse in the city. Conversely, my Dad was in the downturn of the radiation treatment he had received for his lung cancer but continued to push through each day that God sent his way. I admired my Dad's strong constitution despite his discomfort. One of the few pleasures he found joy in during his ordeal was his first grandson, Little Pais. I vividly remember Dad holding my son's hand as they would walk up and down the back alleyway of my parents' home. Every time I would see Big Paisley and Little Paisley together, I was so proud that I named my son after his grandfather as a lasting legacy to my father. Other memorable times that I won't forget was when Dad would sit Pais on his lap and let him share the meat on his dinner plate and sip some of his coffee.

My son really enjoyed drinking his grandfather's coffee, but he especially loved eating all of Dad's bacon at breakfast time! Those priceless memories are indelibly etched in my mind.

A month after we celebrated my youngest son's second birthday, I went to see a Washington doctor a girlfriend recommended about a pain I kept having in my lower stomach. It was during that visit that the doctor encouraged me to have my tubes tied in lieu of staying on birth control pills. He said it was a reversible procedure if I later decided I wanted more children. Actually, I wanted to have eight children, but dropped that number to five and ended up settling for just three. At the time the doctor recommended I have a tubal ligation, I had no hopes of getting married again. However, I was comforted by the knowledge that I could at least have the procedure reversed if I were to marry again, and my new husband wanted me to have more children. Given those choices, I consented for Dr. Cromer to do the procedure.

I checked into Doctors Hospital in Washington DC on May 2, 1974. My procedure was scheduled for the next day. When I awoke, I was in a lot of pain. I called my parents to let them know I was okay. I had a strange craving for some pork skins, so I asked my Dad to bring me some when they came to visit. Later that day, my mom, Dad, and sister came to the hospital to visit with me. I asked Dad if he remembered my meat skins, and he nodded his head yes. But before he gave me the bag, he warned me to wait a day before eating those skins because I would have terrible gas pains like I couldn't imagine after having surgery. That warning made no sense to me, so I popped open that bag and devoured those meat skins straight away. Dad looked at me and quietly said, "Vee, you're gonna regret that."

Next my mother lifted the covers, looked at my stomach, and asked me why my lower abdomen was all bandaged up if I was only in the hospital to have my tubes tied. That procedure would have only caused me to have a small Band-Aid over my navel and not my entire lower belly bandaged up. Since I had no clue about what my mother was saying, I couldn't give her an answer, so she made my sister have the doctor paged and demanded to know what he had done to me.

Dr. Cromer gave my parents the full details of my surgery but *never*—I repeat, never—told me those details! He only told me that I had a problem, and he took care of it. Turns out, the reason I was completely bandaged across my abdomen was because Dr. Cromer had removed my uterus without my permission instead of tying my tubes as I had authorized. There I was, a young twenty-eight-year-old woman who no longer was able to have more children through no fault of my own. Man oh man, was I bummed! The explanation the doctor gave my family why he performed a hysterectomy on me was because one of the ligaments that supported my uterus had collapsed, so he took out the uterus because the ligament couldn't be stabilized, so he said. I didn't know then that the doctor's explanation was basically "frackle nackle bull" (as Michael Baisden says). That truth was borne out in the operative report when my *new* doctor requested my medical records from the surgeon. My uterus was not diseased but was still viable and should not have been taken out. I was assured that the collapsed ligament could have been repaired. To add insult to injury, I found out that Dr. Cromer was a proponent of sterilization of African American women. My first regret is that I didn't sue Dr. Cromer for performing an unauthorized surgery and stealing my ability to give birth ever again.

When Dad left the hospital after visiting me (I remembered his parting words about my disobedience over those meat skins like it was yesterday), he said, "Vee, a hard head will make a soft behind." By the way, my Dad was absolutely correct about those meat skins. Later that night, I suffered with the worst pain imaginable from being swollen with some severe gas! I was released from the hospital seven days later. My recovery was slow and painful. During the time I was sick, my job was abolished with the railroad; and I had no income during my recovery. I temporarily panicked over how I would feed my children, then quickly pulled myself together and decided to apply for temporary public assistance until I could find another job.

I made a phone call to the social services department to find out what information I needed to take to their office to apply for aid. The next day, I went to the welfare department and applied for food stamps and financial help. I actually walked into their office with a cane, bent over in pain, and very carefully sat myself down. The counselor who helped me was full of genuine compassion and processed me quickly. My three children and I qualified for a substantial amount of food stamps and public assistance. We were also granted temporary medical aid for ninety days. (That was over thirty years ago when the process was less complicated.) It goes without saying that my recovery went a whole lot smoother knowing that my children would not go hungry and that my rent would be paid while I was out of work.

One of my girlfriends teased me about my surgery. She said the doctor had taken out the crib and left the playpen. That comment was supposed to make me feel better, but it didn't because I was privately mourning over the reality that I could never have another baby. I sulked for a while and then pulled myself together because nothing I did, felt, or said would change the fact that my uterus was no longer in my body; and I would be barren the rest of my life. I refocused all my thoughts on my three healthy children and thanked God that I, at least, had given birth to them before the unauthorized sterilization happened.

One of the agencies I registered with for temporary assignments found me a long-term temporary assignment right down the street from the railroad where I used to work. It was a six-month assignment with the possibility of it becoming a permanent position. I agreed to the terms because I needed the job. I started work in August and canceled the public assistance I was receiving. The workspace I was given made me realize it was a mistake accepting that assignment. The agency put me under contract and sent me to the client company without an interview—the client's decision to accept me as the agency's recommended temp was purely based on my resumé and outstanding work history. When I showed up for work the first day, it was quite obvious they were shocked to see that I was Negro. The looks of surprise on the faces of everyone who saw me were not at all subtle. I had seen that look many times. My desk was placed in the back of the file room, in the corner behind a whole bunch of tall file cabinets clearly out of sight for anyone coming into the office and seeing me. Despite that, I made the best of the situation because it was a good-paying job. I promised myself that when the last day of my six-month contract came, I would go to lunch and not come back. I really hated that job, but my hands were tied and I couldn't quit because I would have to pay a hefty termination fee to the agency if I left before my contract expired.

That next month during the Labor Day weekend, my Dad called me at work and asked me to drive him to his next doctor appointment because he was feeling poorly. He had lost his appetite and was losing weight rapidly. The doctor told me that my Dad was in the final stages of his cancer and gave him less than six months to live. Although I was aware of the severity of his condition, I wasn't ready to lose him. We had developed a pretty good relationship over the years, and I wanted him to enjoy his grandchildren for a little while longer. But that was not to be.

I brought Dad home from the doctor's office, helped him up the stairs to his bedroom, and put him to bed. That was the last day my Dad felt the warm sunshine on his face because it was all downhill from there. Since I was still commuting to Washington DC, I had to rearrange my childcare schedule so I could immediately go to my parents' home after work. My evening care of my father was a big help and relief to Mom because it allowed her a short respite from running up and down the stairs while taking care of Dad's daytime needs. While I helped with caring for our sick father, my wonderful sister agreed to help each day by picking up my three children from their day care, taking them home, feeding them, helping with their homework, and putting them to bed while I remained with our Dad. Dee is not comfortable around sick people because she feels powerless to make them feel better. And seeing our Dad in the condition he was in was heartbreaking for her. Nevertheless, we completely understand each other enough to know that I am a caregiver and she is not, so there was no disagreement with the roles we had while our Dad was sick. My sister played an extremely important part in the sharing of responsibility during our Dad's sickness. Both of us had tirelessly long days, but we were definitely a team.

Each evening I would change Dad's bed sheets, replace the chux, scrub the floor, and spoon-feed him his dinner. Since he was still able to get out of bed and move around slowly in his room right up until Thanksgiving Day, Dad insisted on using the bathroom on his own albeit feebly and slowly done. During the time I spent with Dad during the Thanksgiving holiday, he reminded me not to forget to tell him how much money I needed for the children's Christmas toys that year. He mentioned that he had put my name on his checking account, and I could write the check myself. I thanked him and decided to wait until Christmas was closer before accepting Dad's check.

The first week of December, I had a strange premonition; I kept calling my supervisor Sybil—her name was Tish. Immediately, I prepared myself for *something* to happen. The morning of December 11, 1974, my mother called to tell me that Dad wasn't doing well; he wouldn't eat, and he was very restless. I called my sister to tell her what was happening and left work two hours early to go straight to my parents' home. I raced up the stairs and walked into Dad's room. He was lying in his bed with a really strange look in his eyes. Although his voice was a whisper now, he told me he needed to go to the bathroom. I helped him out of bed and held on to him as he struggled to get to the toilet. I thought to myself, *How brave he is to push himself instead of using a bedpan.* While Dad was on the commode, I quickly changed his bed. Dad tapped weakly on the door to get my attention. When I opened the bathroom door to see if he was ready for me to help him back to bed, I noticed he was breathing real hard and labored. He had rested his emaciated little arm on the sink, which was right next to the toilet, and I thought he was collecting himself before letting me lift him up. However, Dad would not let me lift him but motioned for me to lean in close to his face. So I leaned over, put my ear in front of his mouth, and heard him whisper, "Vuanita, I love you." (Dad only called me by my middle name when he really wanted to get my attention.) That was the first time I heard my Dad say he loved me.

I stood up straight, readying myself to lift Dad up off the toilet, but he looked up at me, made a gurgling sound, and dropped his head after breathing his last breath. My Dad had just died, and I had to figure out what to do next. I called out to my mother and sister who were downstairs standing at the bottom of the staircase. I told them, "He's gone." Neither my mom nor sister wanted any part of helping me with dad's dead body that night. So I asked my sister to take my children home because it would be a long night for me, and I asked my mom to call the police. Although I knew my father's death was inevitable, I had a unique *Oh! Jesus* moment facing me. My dilemma was figuring out how to get Dad off that toilet and back onto his bed until the Coroner came to pronounce him.

Before that night, I had always been afraid of dead people. But incredibly, I was not afraid of my Dad's corpse. I guess me knowing that the responsibility was resting on my shoulder to clean him up caused my adrenaline to kick in. I said a quick prayer asking God's help and an amazing state of calm came over me along with the wherewithal of what to do next. I went back into Dad's room and pulled the covers all the way down on his bed so I could cover him up once I got him back in his bed. Then I went over to my Dad sitting on the commode, and braced myself as I positioned one arm under his knees, slid one arm around his back, and lifted him up off the toilet. As I lifted my knee to push him upward by his butt so I wouldn't drop him, I suddenly remembered—while standing on one trembling leg—that his bottom was soiled with loose stool, and I didn't want to get any of it on my new knit pantsuit. So I lowered my leg down on the floor and struggled to carry my Dad back into his room. (Deadweight is really heavy.) Fortunately, God heard my pleas and empowered me to not drop my Dad but safely get him back to his bed.

Next I cleaned him off, tied his chin up with a handkerchief to close his mouth, and placed two pennies on his eyes to keep them shut. (I had seen that done in a movie, so I knew what to do for a dead body until the Coroner arrived.) I did not pull the covers over my Dad's face but just up to his chin because I wanted to see his face as long as I could before he was taken away to the morgue. He looked as if he was sleeping. Several hours had passed since the police were called and the Coroner finally arrived, pronounced him, put Dad in a body bag, and took him away. Although I felt sad about my Dad's death, I did not cry that night at his passing. The next day, I helped my mother make the funeral arrangements.

A week before Dad died, he had given me his checkbook to do some Christmas shopping for his grandchildren. His checkbook showed $832 in his account. The worst argument I ever had with my mother was over that $832. She demanded that I go to the bank, close the account, and give her all the money. I told her that Dad had wanted to help me with my children's Christmas shopping, but I didn't get it done before he died. I went on to tell her that I would give her the remaining money after I took out $100 for Christmas. My mother emphatically told me not to take any of *her husband's money*, but to give her that $832 immediately. I went to the bank that same day because I was really angry with my mother for the selfish, money-grubbing attitude she showed me. To my surprise, Dad had made a $300 deposit back in September when he fell sick but forgot to write it in his checkbook. So instead of there being $832 in the account, the balance was $1,132. I closed the account, gave my mother "her" $832, and kept the rest.

In Dad's memory, my children had their best Christmas that year.

23

Veni, Vidi, Vici

To live we must conquer incessantly,
we must have the courage to be happy.

—Henri Frédéric Amiel (1821-1881)

I started a new job that January and thought I was okay over the recent loss of my father, but later discovered that I wasn't. I didn't mourn or cry over Dad's death until six months later. I went into a card store to buy a Father's Day card when suddenly, it hit me that my Dad was not here anymore. I ran out of the store to my car, sat there, and boohooed something terrible for two hours. I realized I missed the sense of comfort I got when I went to him to fix one of my financial dilemmas or just for some fatherly advice; that part of my life was gone. Although Dad never spoke of, or apologized for, his part in the loss of my first child, I believed he tried to make it up to me in other ways absent a verbal apology—like rescuing me every time I called him about a spat I had with Sack, or buying the furniture for my very first apartment, or making sure my children had a good Christmas. I just missed seeing his face. I was no longer Daddy's little girl, so I had to put on my *big-girl panties* and get on with my life.

That summer, I moved out of the city into a brand-spanking-new apartment complex in the county that my sister found for me. I moved on the average of every two years because I enjoyed moving into *new* apartments. The rooms were larger, all the appliances were new, and the children had safer surroundings in which to play. I quickly found my way around to the neighboring supermarkets and shopping malls in my new community. The street blocks were really long, and my children enjoyed riding their bikes up and down the sidewalks. The neighborhood was quiet, and the neighbors that I met seemed friendly enough. One very handsome neighbor, in particular, was especially friendly toward me whenever I was outside with the children; but I attributed his friendliness to him being *gay* since he had a male roommate. However, I started wondering about my assumption of their lifestyle after seeing parades of different women going in and out of their apartment. I thought, *Perhaps they were the neighborhood stud*s. In any event, I wasn't interested in validating my theory and tried minding my business and not looking in the direction of their apartment building whenever I was outside.

One beautiful Saturday morning in July, I let the children go outside briefly, without me, to play and ride their bikes in front of our apartment. Pam, my oldest, was eight years old and good with watching out for her younger brothers. However, this particular Saturday, Pam and Paisley were riding their bikes; and three-year-old Phillip was trailing behind, trying really hard to keep up with his older siblings. When I turned away to answer the phone and looked back out of my window to see where the children were, I saw my neighbor carrying my three-year-old son in his arms, walking to my front door. Phillip was crying and holding on to the man for dear life. Running behind my neighbor were my other two children. I quickly ended my call and ran to the door.

I opened my front door, looked at my neighbor, and asked, "What's going on?" He immediately introduced himself as Tom and told me that Phillip had fallen off his little tricycle and started crying because his brother and sister had left him and were way down the street, so he thought he'd comfort Phillip and take him to his mommy. I thanked Tom and invited him inside. Pam and Paisley ran in behind Tom to see if Phillip was okay, and once they found out he was, they went back outside. Tom handed me Phillip; I wiped away his tears and asked him if he was okay. He showed me his boo-boo. I kissed it and put a Band-Aid on his leg, and off he ran down our short hallway to play in his room. While Tom was standing there, I took notice at the way he stared at me—not like a gay guy should be looking at a woman, but like a man would look at a woman. Suddenly, I felt self-conscious and confused about the look. However, that confusion quickly disappeared when Tom commented on how pretty my eyes were.

Looking at him up close like that was exhilarating. First of all, he had the prettiest white teeth I had ever seen on a man, and I couldn't take my eyes off his mouth. His perfect teeth were nestled behind two thin lips, emphasized with a perfectly trimmed mustache. *I even joked with him that his teeth were so pretty that he could do a commercial for a dentist.* Second, his voice was warm and soothing, which I likened to warm honey. Third, he was tall, tan, and an amazing piece of eye candy. For a split second, I was lost in awe of that beautiful creature. I quickly snapped back to my senses, refocused my glance out the window, and thanked him for bringing my baby home to me. As I opened the door to let him out, Tom turned toward me and commented that he'd like to see me again. I blushed and demurely said, "Perhaps."

I couldn't wait for him to leave before I dashed to the phone to call Dee. *She is always the first person I call whenever anything interesting happens to me or I need my big sister's counsel.* I immediately told her about meeting my next-door neighbor, how handsome and charming he was, and the fact that he said he'd like to see me again. It had been about six months since I had dated, and the possibility of Tom being a new prospect intrigued me. Dee could tell from the excitement in my voice that the wheels of pursuit were turning inside my brain about this man. She joked with me that Tom didn't have a clue what was about to hit him.

My sister Dee is the more stable one between us. She was a devoted and long-time employee for forty-two years in her last job, not fickle like me who changed jobs every two or three years. She was also a devoted and long-time companion when she was in a relationship. Whereas I didn't possess those qualities but grew bored with the same partner. Despite all my escapades, I could always count on Dee to patiently listen to my adventures. I was very happy for my sister when she and her long-time beau were expecting a baby girl that November, and I looked forward to being an auntie. In the meantime until that blessed event, I decided it was time for me to get myself a new playmate.

That next Wednesday, as the kids and I were getting out of our car, Tom pulled up in his car also after presumably getting off from work. The children ran over to him, and he hugged each of them. Little Phillip, however, didn't want to let go of his pants leg, so I had to coax him away from Tom. I tried to hurry and walk away, but Tom stopped me and asked if I had decided yet whether I would go out with him. Cornered, I had to give him an answer; so I said, "Sure, I'd like that very much, so why don't you pick the date and tell me what time I should be ready!"

To which Tom replied, "You've got yourself a deal, pretty lady." He asked me for my phone number, and after giving it to him, I gathered my children and went indoors.

Tom didn't waste any time calling me about that date! Friday, he called to tell me to be ready 7:30 Saturday night because he was taking me out to dinner. I arranged for a sitter, was dressed to kill, and ready to greet Tom on time. My intention was to dazzle him; instead, when I opened my front door, there stood a six-foot-tall bar of scrumptious chocolate. His cologne briefly hypnotized me, and I had to shake myself to regain my wits. The restaurant Tom selected was outstanding, and the food was divine. We talked for hours and shared lots of things about ourselves to each other. I learned that his zodiac sign was Pisces (that's when I knew I was in trouble); he had been married twice before, never had children but would consider getting married again if he met the right woman, was from Detroit, and had two siblings. I shared with him similar things about myself, told him about Phillip's birth, confessed that I had not gotten a divorce from my husband because it had not been an issue for either of us during the eight years we had been separated. However, if I met the right man, I too would consider doing it again. After spending such a blissful evening with Tom, I knew he was not the kind of man I wanted as my teddy bear; he was definitely someone I'd prefer an exclusive relationship with. So I decided to make him mine.

Our friendship grew deeper, and we quickly found ourselves spending a lot of time together. After four dates with Tom, I discovered he *definitely* was not gay. In fact, we had such amazing chemistry until I think I became addicted to him. His voice, his touch, his prowess, and his endurance were just some of the ingredients of the whirlwind romance we had. Pretty soon, we acted and looked like an ideal family.

November rolled around, and my sister gave birth to a beautiful curly haired little princess. Me-me was the apple of Dee's eye. From the moment my niece could walk, I saw genetics at work firsthand because my niece had my attitude and sassy side. As she grew, it was obvious that Me-me had her mother's brains because she was a little genius. Tom loved children and especially loved playing with the little ones in the family—Me-me and Phillip. As our relationship grew stronger, Tom started talking about getting married and how we'd need a larger apartment. I didn't pay too much attention to those conversations because we had only been dating less than a year, and marriage was the last thing on my mind. However, during my birthday weekend in 1976, Tom proposed to me. I was shocked and surprised, but said yes.

That next week, I contacted my cousin, a lawyer, and asked him to file for my divorce from Sack. Next I located a three-bedroom apartment and made arrangements to move in September. Until I knew for sure when my divorce would be final, Tom and I couldn't set a date for our marriage ceremony, but we knew we wanted it to be in a few months. I bought a blue dress for my wedding and outfits for the children. Tom wanted to adopt Phillip as his son, so I asked Sack to grant permission so we could begin the adoption process. Sack was outraged at the request. He refused and made it clear to me that Phillip was still his son even though not his biological child. I never brought up the subject again. Tom and I had put together most of the details for our marriage; all we needed was for my divorce to be final. To my surprise and delight, Tom asked if, in the meantime, he could take me on our pre-wedding honeymoon. I agreed, and off we went to Acapulco for seven days. We had a blast there until the seventh day when both of us came down with Montezuma's revenge. Tom actually had to see his doctor when we returned home for medication to stop his diarrhea. Other than that, we enjoyed ourselves.

Shortly after moving into the three-bedroom apartment that would be our new home once we were married, I had a riveting dream about my dad in early September of 1976.

> In the dream, I saw my Dad in a tuxedo, sitting in a room with a large group of other men in tuxedos. One of his favorite television cowboy actors who played the Rifleman, Chuck Connors, was standing in front of this large group of men, talking to them. Tom and I were standing in the lobby of the reception hall, waiting to get on the elevator to go upstairs and make our wedding arrangements. Just before stepping into the elevator, I looked inside the large room and saw my Dad standing up, looking at me, shaking his head from left to right in a gesture that meant no.

I knew that dream was a message from my Dad telling me not to marry Tom. When I awoke the next morning, I called Tom, told him we couldn't get married at that time, and broke the engagement.

Tom immediately rushed over to my apartment to find out why I had changed my mind. Of course, I couldn't tell him *a warning from my Dad in a dream* was the reason I called off the wedding, so I simply said I had cold feet and didn't want to act too hastily. I tried giving Tom his ring back, but he wouldn't take it and told me to hold on to it until I changed my mind. He said he understood my anxiety and was willing to wait. For the next two months, Tom courted me relentlessly and finally wore me down until I changed my mind about marrying him. Ironically, after agreeing again to marry him, my lawyer called to tell me that my divorce was final and signed by the judge on December 4, 1976. Tom and I set our wedding date for December 11, 1976—the anniversary of my Dad's death. No doubt, Tom's persistent efforts to change my mind clearly made me forget the warning my Dad gave me in the dream I had a few months back.

Our ceremony was private with just immediate family. Tom's mom, brother, and sister flew in from Detroit. Once again, for the second time, my mother did not attend my wedding. Our marriage was quaint, tasteful, and quite beautiful. My seven-year-old son gave me away while my four-year-old son made faces at his brother to make him laugh. My daughter, Pamela, was such a pretty flower girl. However, the minister was an hour late getting to our apartment because he got lost, and Little Paisley was a wee bit frightened about walking beside me with everyone staring at him; but otherwise, the ceremony went off without a hitch. The children were elated they now had a "Dad" in the home.

A week into the marriage when I was working on our budget, my dream about Dad came crashing back into my memory. Before we were married, Tom and I discussed our finances and decided to pool both our paychecks into one account. (Not a good idea.) I wrote the checks to pay our bills, gave the checks to my husband for him to sign, sealed and stamped the envelopes to go in the mail the next day. For the next two weeks, Tom was impotent and couldn't understand what was wrong since we had not had problems in the bedroom before. He said he would see a doctor, but I wasn't convinced he had a medical problem, so I started going through my mind trying to figure out what was different between us since getting married. Then it hit me—*Tom didn't like giving up his paycheck, which was a huge symbol of his independence.* So to test my theory, I suggested that he keep his paycheck, pay his own bills, I pay mine, and that we each only pool half of our joint debt like the rent, utility, and phone bills. Why was I not surprised when his virility returned, with a vengeance no less, once he was again in control of his paycheck? The lesson learned there was an eye opener for me.

Over the coming months, I recognized that my husband's financial prowess was seriously lacking and not one of his strengths. He couldn't balance his checkbook and continually bounced checks. Consequently, he came up short on his half for the household pool we agreed on. Clearly, I earned a lower salary as a secretary than my husband's UPS income, but I regularly covered the shortfalls because that's what marriage is all about—holding each other up. Right? Tom was an absolutely wonderful father figure to my children. When I had to work late, he'd feed, bathe, and tuck my kids in at bedtime; and he would place a mint on my pillow along with the nightie he wanted me to put on when I came to bed. Tom was the epitome of a romantic, and I loved that quality in him, but I was guilty of not appreciating him for those good qualities he brought to our marriage. Instead, I focused on, and grew increasingly disenchanted with, all the things he couldn't do. I had lofty and unreasonable expectations of my husband.

The demise of my marriage to Tom came after I read a book entitled *Looking Out for Number One* by Robert Ringer. Thirteen months into our marriage, I came home from work one day and told my husband that I didn't want to be married anymore. He looked at me in astonishment and reminded me that *we weren't dating anymore—we were married!* He went on to declare that he was not a perfect soul, but a work in progress and suggested that I should be more understanding of his shortcomings. Moreover, he insisted that he loved the children and me but had difficulty coping with my inflexibility and controlling ways. Despite that, he didn't want to give up on our marriage and asked that I not give up on us either.

The place I was in at that time was what I have since identified as a "me, myself, and I" mode. I wanted what I wanted, when I wanted it, and had no tolerance for anything less. Telling Tom that I didn't want to be married to him any longer was clearly because I wasn't capable of accepting him as he was, but consistently tried making him into someone that he wasn't.

The second regret of my life is that I let a good man get away because I was too stupid and self-centered to recognize or realize as well as embrace the good qualities Tom had. Instead, I chose to let his shortcomings cloud my judgment and shut down our marriage. A popular minister in Texas describes that scenario as the 80/20 rule—one gives up 80 percent of a good situation because the not-so-good 20 percent of their situation is what the focus is on. The 80/20 rule is what was at play in my mind and the basis for my decision to end the marriage.

Two months after pronouncing my desire to not be married any longer, Tom reluctantly moved out of our home into his own apartment.

24

The Richness of Humility

Life is a long lesson in humility.

—James M. Barrie (1860-1937)

Here I was alone again; only this time, the tinge of regret I had was completely because I did not pay closer attention to my dream when Dad warned me not to marry Tom. We all know that hindsight is 20/20 vision, but looking through the rearview mirror of a circumstance does not relieve one of the consequences that come with a bad choice. I thought I was smart enough to see the train wreck I was about to have. Trying to pick up the pieces of my failed marriage made me know that regardless of your age or how smart you think you are, everybody plays the fool sometimes.

Six months had passed since Tom and I separated. However, while we were together, I used my credit cards to fund Tom's indulgences because his credit was jacked up. Sadly, he left me with a lot of debt that I could not manage after my household went from two incomes down to one. I was now in dire straits, over my head in debt, and unable to single-handedly maintain the household basics and the credit card payments; so I had to file for bankruptcy. It was devastating for me to stand up in federal court and admit, under oath, that I could not pay my bills. As I left the courthouse that day, I reminded myself that I must not be afraid of one more circumstance that caused me pain nor should I look back or run and hide. I had already put on my big-girl panties when my Daddy died; so I had to suck up my pride, stop beating myself up over another failed marriage, and keep stepping because *this too shall pass*.

On September 19, an indelible event happened that is forever etched in my brain as a wholesome example of just how God never gives up on us regardless of how not so good we think we are. I went to the store to get some medicine because the kids and I had very bad colds. I was hoarse and sounded horrible, and they were coughing and sneezing like crazy. While standing there trying to make up my mind which cold medicine to buy—because I only had enough money to buy just one—a disheveled and slightly inebriated man walked up beside me and started a general conversation about all the different varieties of cold medicine there were on the shelf and how we, as consumers, are clueless about which one is the best. I told him how my children and I had bad colds, and I was trying to decide which medicine would work for all of us. I felt lousy, was constantly blowing my red nose, but didn't want to be rude to the fella; so I kept making small talk while trying to walk away from him. He told me his name was Rimp and asked me mine. I told him Vee and once again tried walking away, but he just wouldn't leave me alone. Then he said I looked cute with my red nose! That's when I knew he was hitting on me. Admittedly, my pride made me look at him sideways because, ordinarily, I would not have considered a man in his state as someone of interest. Although his speech was slurred from too much to drink and he rocked back and forth a little, there was a distinct humbleness about him that I could not ignore.

Rimp asked me if I would permit him to buy the cold medicine for the children and me because he wanted us to get well—and see me again. I stood there dumbfounded because I'd never heard that pickup line before; I wasn't sure if he was a nut, a really nice guy disguised as my knight in rusted armor, or an angel that I was about to pass judgment on. Knowing I only had enough money for one bottle of cough medicine but really needed several different medicines to make us well, I decided Rimp had to be an angel that God placed on my path to help me that day. I accepted his offer, gave him my phone number, and chose $22.65 worth of cold medicine. Rimp paid the cashier with his American Express Card, promised to check on me the next day, and waved goodbye as I drove out of the parking lot. That strange encounter in Read's Drugstore that day was the beginning lesson that God would teach me on humility in its purest form.

Just as he promised, Rimp called me the next evening to check on me and also see how the kids were doing with their colds. We had a long conversation that day and every day afterward for the next two weeks. I had never met a man as sensitive as Rimp nor had I ever allowed myself to consider being with anyone like him. I admit I judged him harshly, but the more we talked, the more convinced I became that I could really get into this guy. It soon was not an issue for me that he wasn't handsome, didn't own a car, was a smoker, a maintenance man, and an alcoholic. He confessed that he was afraid to marry again and had been estranged from his wife for nine years but did not expect them to reconcile. I cannot tell you why I let myself fall for Rimp, but I did. After we had been dating for about three months, I introduced him to my family and my children. Everyone loved him because of his sense of humor and kindhearted ways. Rimp was actually very good for me as well as good to me. The main challenge I had going into this relationship was his weekend drinking. Rimp was a sweet and lovable drunk, which was not the norm, who preferred being around the kids and me at our apartment during the weekend. But when Monday morning rolled around, he was as sober as I was and never missed a day of work because of his drinking.

I knew I was committed to Rimp when there was a knock at my front door one Friday night just before Christmas. Rimp was sprawled out on the floor in the den, sauced to the gills, and was asleep. It was Tom. He stopped by to ask me if I would consider us getting back together and making our marriage work. Shocked, surprised, and speechless, I told him I had moved on with my life; and reconciliation was not something I would consider since my life was different now. Three months later, I was served with divorce papers. I never told Rimp about that Friday-night visit from Tom. However, when the process server delivered my divorce papers, Rimp asked me if I regretted not being married—was I frightened or sad? I immediately told him no, no, and no.

Rimp gave up his apartment and moved in with the children and me. They were very excited to have him around all the time, especially the boys. He taught my sons manly skills, particularly how to tie a necktie (because I didn't know how to teach them that), and he also taught them to lift the toilet seat up when they had to urinate (because that's how a man does it). Paisley and Phillip enjoyed sparring with Rimp. He taught how to throw a punch. Rimp insisted on teaching my sons how to defend themselves against an encounter with a bully. He also was sensitive to my daughter's love for roller-skating; he took her downtown and bought her very own first pair of roller skates and a carrying bag for her weekly skate nights at the coliseum. The most enlightening thing Rimp taught me was that boys should be disciplined differently than girls. Rimp said it was sissified for me to make my sons wash dishes as punishment. He said I had to give them tougher things as punishment like washing and waxing my car or scrubbing and waxing all the floors in the house. When the boys misbehaved, he helped me come up with different punishment exercises for them instead of the same type of punishment I gave my daughter. That nugget of knowledge really made a difference with my style of discipline.

More importantly, during my entire relationship with Rimp, I learned humility. Many times, during his weekend benders, I had to put him to bed. There were nights I woke up feeling a bone-chilling coldness on the back of my pajamas from where Rimp had wet the bed during his drunken stupors. Other times, when he drank and ate his favorite snack food—hot dogs with huge pieces of onion on the bun—he would throw up all over my baby blue carpets. I regularly cleaned up his mess, with all those big pieces of onion strewn throughout; all the while fussing at him as I scrubbed. Needless to say, he didn't pay attention to me when I fussed him out. Actually, he just kept repeating how much he loved me!

Rimp told me about a higher-paying position at work that he wanted. Every day for two weeks, I encouraged him to apply for the job and reminded him that he could do whatever he put his mind to. I continually pushed him to rise higher and keep striving for better. When I met Rimp, his good qualities did not come shining through at the outset. But they were there. No surprise to me that Rimp got the job! My next challenge was to encourage Rimp to take a higher step and buy himself a car. I believed he could achieve that goal but I had to convince him that he could. After receiving the promotion, he then earned enough money to afford a car payment, so I constantly talked to him about buying himself a car. Finally, he said yes and asked me to drive him to a local dealership to see what would happen. After spending three hours at the dealership, Rimp drove out of the dealership in his own brand-new Chevette. That day, he was so proud of himself in a way I have never seen before. I was concerned, however, that his drinking might be a problem for him now that he was behind the wheel of a car. My next challenge was to help him *want to* stop drinking. I knew I couldn't do that for him; he had to want sobriety himself.

For exactly two years, I had this recurring dream about my mother:

> *I went to Mom's house to visit, but the front screen door was locked. My instincts told me something was wrong, so I asked the next-door neighbor if I could use her upstairs window to step out on the porch roof to get to my Mom's bedroom window. In the dream, the neighbor agreed, and I went through all the motions to reach Mom's bedroom window. I looked inside her window and saw her sitting on the floor, propped up against her closet door. I immediately raised the window, crawled inside Mom's bedroom, and discovered that she had had a stroke. It looked like she had been sitting there for quite some time. Her speech was garbled, and she was hallucinating about seeing snakes. Then the dream would stop.*

Given my history with dreams, I knew this dream had a bigger meaning than what I understood. The dreams kept coming, and I kept waiting on the true meaning to reveal itself to me.

The apartment we lived in was no longer big enough for our family, and we needed more room. Pam was now a teenager, and Pais and Phillip were fast approaching puberty. I located a nice townhouse approximately six miles down the road from where we lived in Randallstown. I made all the arrangements and scheduled our move-in for September. Rimp paid all the costs for us to move, and also moved into this townhouse with us. The location was ideal, and the place was spacious and beautiful. My cousin helped me plant a tiny vegetable garden in the backyard. Before long, Paisley decided he wanted to start saving money to buy himself a car when he turned sixteen, so he got himself a paper route.

Six months into our new townhouse, I had a mommy meltdown. The kids were taxing my patience and feeling their oats, and Rimp's drinking was also getting to me. What I didn't know was that my hormones were getting wacky, and I seriously needed to see a doctor. Instead, I felt I needed a serious break from my lover and my kids, so I decided to go on a weekend ski trip with a girlfriend and leave the clan at home. As I was driving along the boulevard on my way to pay for my ticket, I had just passed my mother's street when I heard God speak to me and say, "Go to your mother's house!" As I was turning my car around in the middle of the street to go back to my mother's street, I was verbally sparring with God. I told him that I needed to get my ski ticket paid for; reminded him Mom probably wouldn't let me in anyway since she had taken my sister's and my door keys from us. Neither of us could get in the house. Even though I continued murmuring to God, I obediently drove up my Mom's block, parked my car, walked up the front steps, and tried turning the knob to open the screen door. It was locked. Next I heard God speak to me again. This time, he said, "Today is the day." Hearing that, something clicked in my brain, and I completely understood what the dream that I had been having for the past two years meant. Needless to say, I did not take that ski trip. Before this incident, I used to call my mother every day even if she would hang up on me sometimes when she was in one of her peculiar moods. The way I figured it, God allowed me to keep having that recurring dream about my mother as the emotional preparation I would require to effectively step through the paces during the tragedy that was before me.

Instinctively, I knew everything that lay ahead of me. Without emotions, I played the script from my dream to the letter. I rang the next-door neighbor's bell and told her Mom didn't answer and the screen door was locked. I asked her if I could use her upstairs bedroom window to step out on the porch roof to get to my Mom's bedroom window. The neighbor led me upstairs, and I went through all the motions to reach Mom's bedroom window just like in the dream. I looked inside Mom's window and saw her sitting on the floor, propped up against her closet door. I quickly raised her bedroom window, crawled inside, and discovered that my mother had, in fact, had a stroke. Her speech was garbled, and she was hallucinating about seeing snakes. I then called 911 to report my emergency. Next I called my sister to tell her what had happened. She came over right away. On top of my mother's dresser lay her will. The paramedics came quickly, worked on Mom for what seemed like an hour or so, then transported her to the hospital.

Both my sister and I followed the ambulance to the hospital. The doctor confirmed that Mom had a stroke, and her chances for recovery were slim to none. Later that night, Mom slipped into a coma that lasted exactly seven days. I was in between jobs, so I was able to sit by her bedside every day. I combed Mom's hair, talked to her, and sang some of her favorite hymns as she lay motionless in that hospital bed. Dee would come to the hospital at the end of her workday and relieve me. On the seventh day of my mother's coma, which was a Saturday, I made up my mind to speak forgiveness to my mother for the hurt I had carried over the past nineteen years for her role in killing my first son. I put my mouth close to her ear and whispered, "Mama, I forgive you for the part you played in the abortion which caused the death of my child. I must forgive you if I expect God to forgive me of my mistakes, so I release you this day." My mother died that night.

Once again, I had to make funeral arrangements for another parent. My sister let me handle everything because her phobia about the dead wouldn't let her even look in a book of funeral flowers to select something nice for our Mom. We completely understood each other's strengths; I handled the funeral arrangements, and Dee handled the business side of everything. Mom's funeral was especially nice. She was highly esteemed and well thought of by her church family. They let her lay in state so that everyone could pay their respects. That was quite an honor. After the internment, we held a repast at Mom's house for all our remaining aunts, uncles, and friends. Unbeknownst to me, Rimp had secretly carried a shorty in his pocket to the funeral. Just before the repast ended, he was stretched out on my mother's bed—stoned. Following my mother's death, I started attending church regularly, recommitted my life to Christ, and grew increasingly discontented with the live-in lifestyle I had with Rimp. I had grown tired of his drinking and all that came with his behavior, so I began praying for God's help with my situation.

In a way that only God could have intervened, my prayers were heard. One Friday after work, Rimp went out drinking with his buddies. Luckily, he drove himself home without an incident. However, as he sat at the red traffic light waiting to turn into our parking lot, he blacked out before the light could turn green. Ordinarily, when he was out drinking, I would watch from my front window for him to drive up to that stoplight, run out to his car, move him over into the passenger's seat, drive the car into our development, and park it. Sometimes, I'd leave Rimp in his parked car to sleep off his stupor; and other times, I'd help him stumble into the house. But that night, I decided to stop enabling him and let him sit there to see what would happen without my intervention, so I simply watched through the kitchen window.

A police car pulled up behind him. When Rimp didn't turn left when the traffic light turned green, the officer got out of his car, turned his flashlight on, and approached Rimp only to find him passed out at the wheel. When I saw the red-and-blue flashing lights from the patrol car, I knew it was all over. The officer pulled Rimp out of his seat and stood him up. That's when I ran out to Rimp's car and told the officer I would move the car because we lived right there at the light. The officer said he had to arrest Rimp on a DWI. He put him in the patrol car and took him off to jail. Monday morning, Rimp called me from the police station to come pick him up so he could go to work. He was as sober as I was. His trial date was in three weeks. But in an attempt to beat the system, Rimp decided to sign himself into an AA treatment program (for the third time) so he could tell the judge he completed the program and get the charges dropped.

To everyone's delight, Rimp completed the twenty-eight-day AA treatment program and received favor from the court; the ruling he received was probation before judgment. That meant he had to stay out of trouble for eighteen months for the charges to be dropped. I thanked God the program worked this time. Rimp never drank liquor again after that. His family was elated over his accomplishment. His mother gave me the credit for helping her son stop drinking. I told her it was God's plan, not mine. Rimp's personality changed after he stopped drinking. I didn't like the person he became; he was insensitive, coldhearted, and not the fun person I had come to know. Truth be told, I liked the *drunken* Rimp much better. Several months after he was out of rehab, we had a heart-to-heart talk; and I let him know I didn't want to continue living in sin with him and suggested we get married—after all, we had been together for six years. However, I did not expect the response Rimp gave me. He said an immediate no to my suggestion, adding that he had no intention of getting married, and recommended that we go our separate ways. Just like that! Rimp and I ended our six-year relationship and parted as friends.

After my relationship with Rimp was over, I prayed for God's forgiveness for my disobedience and focused on raising my teenagers. I found a second job to make up for the loss of Rimp's financial input to our household and did my best to continue providing a decent lifestyle for my children. Although there were many lean days on that journey—like when we had no food in the fridge, or our lights were turned off, or those times the phone was disconnected because there just wasn't enough money to cover everything—God *always* brought us through those times without fail.

As a single parent, I believed I had to be a stern disciplinarian raising two boys and a daughter. I sure wished I knew then what I know now because I would have given my children things that money can't buy, like lots of hugs and kisses and constant reminders of how gifted, talented, and special they were. Even though I loved my children with every fiber of my being, I didn't know how to show them that love when they outgrew the toddler stage. If only I had known that mothers should do girly things with their daughters, like making cookies and baking cakes, I would have shared more of me with my daughter. Sadly, I didn't know to do those things with my daughter because I did not learn them from my mother; instead, I scolded her once for burning the dinner she prepared as a surprise to me. When I recall making that huge mistake as a parent, first, I feel sad at my ignorance; and secondly, I wished I would have hugged my baby girl tightly and expressed appreciation for her thoughtfulness to cook dinner that night. Somewhere along the road of parenting, I came to believe that I had to teach my children how to be tough and become survivors. I was indeed grateful, however, that Rimp crossed my path and was in our lives for those six years because he, at least, taught my sons things that only a man can teach a boy.

I completely recognized that God blessed me with three wonderful children who never gave me one bit of trouble: My daughter was never boy crazy nor ran the streets. My oldest son never needed reminding to do his homework, and always filled our home with humor. And my youngest son was my second skin—very close to his Mom, sensitive to my needs, and the straight arrow in the family. I wanted them to have a better life than I had growing up, so I made sure when an opportunity presented itself to them, I strongly encouraged them to go for it. In our house, my children heard many speeches from me about *the principle of a thing*. I made a lot of mistakes as a parent raising my children, but there is one thing I know for sure that I did right—and that was helping them come to know the true savior, Jesus Christ.

Billy Graham came to our city during a spring season one year, and just like my mother took me to an Oral Roberts revival meeting, I took my three children to Mr. Graham's crusade so they could also meet "Mr. Jesus." When the altar call was given, Pam, Paisley, and Phillip made their way to the altar and asked Christ to come live in their hearts. From that day until this, I have always known my kids would be okay because they have been equipped to be true overcomers. With Christ as their best friend—just like he is mine—I have no doubt he will help them navigate through all their *Oh! Jesus* moments as well.

25

Grace Changes Everything

I do not at all understand the mystery of grace—
Only that it meets us where we are but does not leave us where it found us.

—Anne Lamott (1954-)

It seems like only yesterday that I held my newborn baby girl in my arms as I tried to grasp the newness of motherhood. Now she was getting dressed to go to her high school graduation. I quietly reflected over her younger years and privately wiped away tears as those memories came rushing into my head. Pamela was a sweet and adorably happy child. My baby girl is now all grown-up, attractive, voluptuous, and ready to experience life. Pam, like me, did not want to go right into college after she graduated but decided to get a good job, make some money, and, perhaps, consider college later. We were running late for the ceremony because we were waiting on the boys to get home from a softball game at school. Pamela was frustrated with them for being late, but at the end of the night, the drama was forgotten as our family celebrated her milestone.

Immediately after graduation, my daughter went right out and started working as a temporary employee to get acclimated as a full time office worker. This experience she would gained was not like when she worked at McDonalds. After working as a temp for a couple of months, Pam set her sights on a full-time job with outstanding benefits at a Fortune 500 company that she wanted to interview with. Since I had taught my children that they could do *anything* they put their minds to, the process of going after that job and getting it did not daunt Pam. She passed all their tests and was hired with the salary she asked for.

While preparing dinner one evening, Pam came in from work, and we started talking about her new position. She told me how much she enjoyed what she did but had one regret. When I asked her what it was, she said she wished she had asked for more money as her starting salary. She felt she had undersold herself because they didn't push back when she asked for what she wanted; because of that, she regretted not upping her starting salary a wee bit. I chuckled to myself when she shared that with me. Apparently, she had forgotten that I sat with her just before her interview and helped her work up a budget; and together, we came up with the salary she should ask for, which covered everything including the monthly payment for the brand-new car she had bought herself. It was a fair salary given her experience and her financial needs. I shared the scripture with her that teaches us about being faithful over a few things before God entrusts us with more. Then I drew the parallel that she should *first* be faithful earning the smaller salary, be a good steward, and wait for God to give her a higher salary. Sure enough, Pam's career with that company blossomed, and she went on to be *entrusted with much more*. The next thing Pam mentioned was her desire to eventually move out into her own apartment within the upcoming year. The crushing reality came into focus that my nest was emptying itself. First, Pam would leave; next, my oldest son would be leaving for college. Although I was excited for my children's success, it was a bittersweet joy.

Paisley, who was quite the scholar, was in his junior year of high school when Pam graduated in 1985; and Phillip was in his last year of middle school. It was one of my *absolutes* that my boys go to college because it was critical that they get a college education, especially as an African American man-child. Paisley was scheduled to graduate in 1987. He was a consistent A/B student and scored well on his PSAT and SAT tests, so I knew he was definitely college material. But there was one hitch; I had no money with which to send him to college. My dilemma was a simple one, but one I could not solve. The one sure thing I did know how to do was to pray about my situation and trust God to make a way for him.

Paisley's class had an awards assembly for the honor students just before the Thanksgiving holiday. His Dad and I sat proudly in the audience, watching our son walk across the stage to collect two scholastic awards. I felt terrible inside that I could not afford to send my accomplished and smart son to college when he clearly deserved to go. At that moment of sadness, I bowed my head and spoke directly to God, saying,

> *"Lord, you blessed me with this child, and you gave him an awesome mind, and I thank you. I want him to go to college, but I have no money to send him. Your Word promises to bless the fruit of my womb. So in the name of your precious son, Jesus, I thank you for making a way for Paisley to go to college. Amen."*

I did not know *how* God was going to work things out, but I knew that he would. I can't tell you where that level of faith came from—perhaps it sprang up from my painful childhood—but I completely trusted my best friend, Jesus Christ, to help me.

During the sophomore year, Paisley played football and baseball. In his junior year, the track-and-field coach asked him to consider running track. He had seen Paisley run a touchdown during a football game the year before and was blown away by his speed. One day early in the semester, Paisley mentioned he was going to try out for the track team. I was quite relieved that he wouldn't be playing football again since I cringed every time a player sacked him. And as a mom, you don't like seeing your kid get hurt. Paisley tried out for the track team in his junior year of high school and made the cut. Turns out, his dad, Sack, was a sprinter in high school and his nickname was *racehorse*. Paisley was a natural runner and began winning most of the races he ran. Paisley's signature event was the 400 mm race. However, he quickly excelled and became the anchor leg in the 4x100 and 4x400 mm events.

What I didn't know at that time was that God was using my son's legs—in answer to my prayer—as the door for him to go to college. Throughout Paisley's first year as a runner, God blessed him with abundant *favor*. Despite that, Paisley really wasn't jazzed about going to college. In fact, he told me he considered being a manager of a McDonald's fast-food store because he knew I didn't have enough money to send him to college and said he was okay with that. However, I explained to him that working at McDonald's was not an option, and it was correct I didn't have enough money to send him to college; but I had prayed, and I knew that God would make a way.

Even though I couldn't write a tuition check, I still filled out all the required college entrance paperwork for Paisley. I also filed my tax returns early because our household financial information needed to be disclosed on those forms. The deadline to file the paperwork was fourteen months before Paisley's graduation, and I met that deadline just in the nick of time! Please understand, I was not *helping God out* by doing the paperwork but merely taking care of *my part* of the process because I believed God was taking care of *his part* of the process to get my son into college.

Our family all went to the local conference and invitational track meets that Paisley participated in. He was especially proud of his aunt for the lunches she packed for us to eat. Her basket was chock-full of sandwiches, fruits, cold drinks, snacks, and other goodies; and sometimes, I would fry up a batch of chicken wings for added protein during those long stretches of time when Paisley was in between events. During the fall and winter, Paisley ran indoor track; and during the spring, he ran outdoor track. He finished his junior year with excellent grades and several medals for a winning streak as a neophyte track star. Paisley was such a big inspiration to his younger brother that Phillip signed up to also run track, and his signature event was hurdles.

A year had passed since my prayer for a miracle, but I kept right on, expecting my breakthrough. School resumed in September, and Paisley returned to the track team. I later found out that sometime between September and October during the first semester of his senior year, college scouts came to several of Paisley's high school track meets to observe his running. They liked what they saw, approached him, and asked him to consider coming to their college because they wanted him on their track team. Next they made arrangements for him and me to visit their campus so Paisley could see the college firsthand. I had never heard of Brown University until someone told me it was one of the big ten Ivy League colleges. The icing on the cake was when Paisley's track coach told me that he had recommended Brown to come to Maryland and take a look at my son's running stats for a scholarship. The scholarship Brown offered was an academic scholarship. When I heard that news, my faith grew even more because admission to Brown is extremely competitive. There was my miracle! God used my son's academic honors as the foundation for that scholarship and his *legs* as the door that made the plan come together!

The buzz Brown University made over Paisley chipped away at his desire to skip college and get a job with McDonald's. Our visit to their campus was impressive. Brown's main campus is located atop College Hill (the most affluent neighborhood in Providence) in the East Side across the Providence River from downtown Providence. My concerns that I was sending my child off to a partying town were relieved when I saw for myself that was not the case. I was in complete awe of the magnitude of the miracle God gave us. He didn't just open *any ole door* for my child to go to college; God opened a crème de la crème door of opportunity for my baby.

After Paisley and I returned from the campus visit, I pulled out my trusty typewriter and typed the Brown's entrance application because I wanted it to look professional and represent Paisley in a good light. I meticulously checked and double-checked every line for possible mistakes and attached all the requested documentation. When it was completed, Paisley signed it; I sealed it and personally took it to the post office—praising God all the way.

When May rolled around, my entire family was anxiously awaiting Paisley's college acceptance packet. He said, "Mom, if a large envelope comes in the mail, that's good news and I got in. But if a small envelope comes, the news isn't good." The day the college information came, there were several surprises. First and foremost, Brown University gave my son a full four-year academic scholarship. The family's portion of the tuition, which was the part I had to pay, was a manageable amount that God knew I could handle! Second, there was another scholarship offer to Paisley from Villanova University in Pennsylvania but was not as comprehensive as Brown's offer. Paisley respectfully turned down their scholarship.

The school year came to a glorious close for Paisley, culminating with his spectacular graduation. Watching a second child walk across the stage to receive their high school diploma was one of many joys I experienced that year. Everyone in our family was so proud of Paisley for his accomplishments. I had to learn *restraint* in the full sense of the word when Paisley's Dad bragged about *his son* going to Brown University. It was very hard for me to bite my lip and hush up, knowing that his $15-a-week child-support payments to Paisley had stopped arriving many, many years ago. God had been *our source*, and I knew it was prideful of me to begrudge my ex the joy of seeing his son go to college and take some of the credit for making it happen. How dare he forget what part he *actually* played in all this! The struggles I overcame while raising my three angels were purely because God brought me through all of them and definitely not because my ex shared equally in the financial responsibility for Paisley's care.

When summer was almost over, two major things happened. Number one: my daughter decided it was time for her to move out into her very own apartment. Our family rallied, helped her pack, and moved her into her new dwelling. Second, the time came to send Paisley on his way to Providence, Rhode Island. My sister's huge financial assistance helped us pull together all the things Paisley needed for college. He left for Brown the last weekend in August 1987. Seemingly overnight, my nest emptied itself of two of my three crows (as Tom affectionately called my children) and left sixteen-year-old Phillip.

Paisley called home sporadically, and I missed seeing my daughter's face the first thing every morning. It was quite an adjustment for me to go from a bustling home with constant noise, music, voices, and activity to a predictable calm. Phillip became my new best friend, so to speak. I started a new job (yep, another one) in September working for a large prestigious law firm downtown. I enjoyed going to work every day. The office was beautifully decorated, and I had state-of-the-art equipment to use, which was a treat.

Four months later, it was Christmas. Paisley came home for the holiday break, and he and Phillip went right back to their brotherly groove of cracking each other up with gut-wrenching laughter and staying up late nights sharing their stories of conquests. It was automatic that my home once again filled up with noise, music, and constant activity. Paisley resumed his habit of tying up the telephone with back-to-back lengthy calls to all his friends—especially the ladies. When break was over, he went back to school, and Phillip and I rolled back into our quiet lifestyle.

In March of 1988, my phone rang, and it was a former boss that I had worked for three years prior. Aside from being glad to hear from him, I was curious why he was calling me at home. Dr. Hill told me that he had just been appointed president of a new company in Hillsborough and that he wanted me to come work for him again as his executive assistant. He shared with me the conversation that he had with his wife when he was offered the job. He asked her, What should I do Dixie? And she said, "Call Ronii."

I congratulated him on his new position, told him I would be delighted to work for him again, and asked where Hillsborough was. Then Dr. Hill told me Hillsborough was in North Carolina, and the company would relocate my family if I accepted the job. Oh, and the topping on the dessert was when he said, "And, Ronii, you can write your own ticket." For a second, I didn't know what to say since taking the job would require me to leave all my family and move to North Carolina. I had never lived any place but Baltimore or been that far away from my family. I told Dr. Hill I would call him back after I discussed it with my son.

Dr. Hill was the best *corporate* manager I ever had during my (then) twenty-one-year career. He valued my opinion, appreciated me immensely, and never missed an opportunity to sing my praises to his colleagues. He trusted me implicitly and gave me glowing evaluations for the three years I supported him and his staff. Actually, Dr. Hill had given me high raises two years in a row, which caused me to be in a red circle status—that meant there was no more money in my salary band for another increase. So I worked for Dr. Hill another year without a raise until he was promoted and left the company. Given my history with him, there was no question that I would work for him again; the only issue I had was *moving to another state*.

North Carolina wasn't a completely foreign place for me to live because both of my parents were from there. Actually, Dee and I spent several summers in Carolina with my mother's parents where we learned to ride a bicycle on our grandparents' farm. Since my decision about the job would affect Phillip more than his siblings, I sat down with him and discussed the situation in as much detail as I could. Phillip said, "Mom, go for it!" He added that it would be a new start for me, and I should not let the opportunity pass me by. I called Dr. Hill back the next day and told him I would accept the job. He wanted me to start in May and recommended that he fly us to Carolina so we could find an apartment as soon as possible. Phillip and I flew to Chapel Hill that next weekend and looked at five different apartment complexes. I selected a lovely two-bedroom apartment in Chapel Hill, quit my job in Maryland, and moved into the apartment the last weekend in April. I bought Phillip a little car before leaving Maryland so he could easily get back and forth to school as well as other places he needed transportation to and from. I started working the first week of May, however when the Ku Klux Klan marched through Hillsborough my first week on my new job, I seriously questioned whether I had made the right decision to move to North Carolina. Dr. Hill assured me that everything would be okay, and their march was nothing to worry about.

The company agreed to move my entire household in June once Phillip finished his junior year in Baltimore. Until then, the company flew me back to Baltimore every other weekend and flew Phillip to North Carolina on the alternating weekends. I didn't mind that my living arrangement in North Carolina was bare bones because I knew my furniture would be delivered the next month. The first weekend Phillip came to see me in Carolina, he fell in love with our new home, the state of North Carolina, and was excited about our new life in the South.

Phillip was an exceptional sixteen-year-old whom I trusted completely. It was an easy decision for me to agree to let him stay in the apartment for the six weeks left in his school year because he was my straight-arrow child. There was no doubt in my mind that Phillip could handle himself responsibly in my absence during those 6 weeks left in his school year. He assured me he would not have company in the apartment and would be on his best behavior. We spoke by phone several times a day and saw each other every weekend. I alerted my downstairs neighbor, who was retired, of our commuter situation and asked her to keep an eye out for Phillip during the week. My daughter also checked on her brother to make sure he behaved himself, did his laundry, and kept the house straight. During one of my weekend trips to Baltimore, my downstairs neighbor stopped me in the hallway to tell me how impressed she was with Phillip. She praised him for being extremely mature for his age, respectful and always polite, commenting that he was quiet over her head and never once did she see Phillip let anyone into the apartment. I thanked her for the kind words and immediately shared with Phillip what she said. I was so proud of him for how well he managed without me during his last six weeks of school.

Once the semester was over for Phillip, we moved to Chapel Hill, North Carolina. This was the first time in my life that I didn't have to pack or lift a box. My new employer paid Atlas Van Lines to do all that for us. Phillip and I drove ourselves to Carolina, and the moving van delivered our furniture three days later. I was absolutely elated when I was able to sleep in my own bed instead of that sleeping bag I used while I had no furniture. Phillip enrolled in the local high school and completed his senior year there. He made lots of friends and enjoyed our new lifestyle. After Phillip graduated high school, he got a job as a waiter and enjoyed his summer.

The year prior to Phillip's graduation, I repeated the college paperwork process for Phillip just as I did for Paisley. Because I was a resident of North Carolina, the college tuition for Phillip was manageable, and he was accepted into the University of North Carolina at Chapel Hill. However, thirteen months into my new job, the proverbial rug was snatched out from under me. Dr. Hill and thirteen sales associates were fired. The reason given for the firing was that Dr. Hill was brought in to return the company to a profitable status, and he didn't make that happen. Because he was my insulation, and was now gone, I clearly felt like the *outsider* that I was viewed as and resigned my position four months after the firings. There I was, flapping in the wind one more time. Fortunately, I was familiar with this drill because surviving was something I knew a little something about.

I had two boys in college, and I was their sole support, so I had to push past the defeat I felt and find another job. Getting the salary I had given up was quite another matter. I registered with four temp agencies and combed the want ads in between the temp assignments I worked. It was a hard reality for me that I had taken a 65 percent cut in my pay. I had to decide whether to move back to Baltimore so I could earn a much more reasonable salary than what I was getting or stay in North Carolina and make the best of my situation. I decided the latter. To augment my standard 40 hour work week, I found a twenty-hour weekend job at a local hospital in their admitting office. I worked a ten-hour shift on Saturday and Sunday. Needless to say, there was no time for a social life or anything else for that matter, and I really missed attending church. I worked seven days a week for two straight years, only taking time off for critical matters.

God's grace allowed my weekend partner to be a very funny lady named Sharon. Her unique humor helped me through each and every weekend with crazy gut-wrenching laughter. She was my sunshine. I truly believe that laughter is better than medicine. Not once during those twenty-four months working in that hospital did I ever catch a cold or get sick. I attributed my good health to God's goodness and the miracle of laughter.

After Paisley graduated from Brown in May of 1992, I decided to lighten my work schedule and give up my weekend job. The following weekend I returned from Paisley's graduation, I stood up at my desk during my next weekend shift and made four pronouncements to Sharon: (1) I would turn in my two weeks' notice on June 20, (2) I would meet a man, (3) I would fall in love (*so I thought*), and (4) I would get married.

July 4, 1992, was my last day working that weekend job.

26

Be Careful What You Ask For

*Things that are done, it is needless to speak about . . .
things that are past, it is needless to blame.*

—Confucius

Self-fulfilling prophecies are real because words have power. Scripture says, "The tongue has the power of life and death," and I learned another hard lesson about words I've let come out of my mouth.

Ironically, the week after my four pronouncements to Sharon, an acquaintance that I met when I first moved to North Carolina called me, once again, to tell me about one of his employees that he believed would be a good match for me. Up until that day, I had continually refused his attempts to introduce me to the man. However, that day I was not feeling well, his insistence wore me down; and I agreed to meet the person he told me about just so my friend would stop bugging me. Next he handed the phone over to the gentleman. He said his name was Ed, and I told him mine. We talked briefly before he pressed me about us meeting each other. Apparently, my friend had sung my praises to the man and piqued his curiosity. I agreed to meet him that following Saturday and gave him my home address.

On July 25, 1992, my doorbell rang, and I opened the door to see a handsome shorter-than-I-preferred caramel-colored man standing there. I invited him in, and we talked for hours. I immediately liked his mind although I thought I might be a wee bit too aggressive and brazen for him. He was very much a gentleman and very respectful. We talked to each other about ourselves, albeit laced with discretion about what we disclosed to each other that night. I began to feel inferior to him because of his educational and professional accomplishments. As a little distraction, I decided to kiss him before the night was over since stoking lustful fires was something I did well. After talking for several hours, we moved from sitting on the couch to sitting on the floor.

The next thing I did was intended to scare Ed away. I turned to him and told him I was going to kiss him after we chewed a piece of gum to freshen our breath. I finish my gum first, so I straddled his lap and kissed him gently on his mouth. Much to my amazement, he was not put off by my aggression but was quite responsive to my advances. I assessed him as what I call a Sleeper—that is, someone who looks cold and indifferent on the surface but once engaged, is quite the fireball inside. Beginning with those passionate moments of us rolling around on my living room floor, we recognized we had good chemistry together. Let me be clear about one thing. I did not ask God to send me this man, nor did I pray about whether I should embark on a relationship with him. Once again, I totally allowed my flesh to lead me.

At the time we met, I had been divorced from husband number 2 for fourteen years and had not been seriously involved with anyone for about four years. Ed was also divorced twice but didn't disclose any other information about a recent relationship. We had several phone conversations over the next several days, and our first date was two weeks later. Ed took me for a walk through the Duke Botanical Gardens. I thought that was very boring but indulged him since I left it up to him how we would spend our first date. Several more times, he visited me at my home, and I behaved myself. After we had dated for about three weeks, the next time Ed came over, I jumped his bones—and he let me.

After we came to know each other (in the biblical sense of the word), we saw each other regularly during the weekends. He usually spent Thursday, Friday and Saturday at my house. I would even get up at 4 A.M. and fix him breakfast and pack his lunch for work. Two months into our relationship, I met some of his family. I was almost a dead ringer for his mom; she also had a birthday in July and was feisty like me. I especially enjoyed the relationship I had with his sister-in-law right up until the day she died. Let me just say that Ed was a really nice guy; but we were wrong for each other. If I were smarter at that time, I would not have allowed my relationship with Ed to become as serious as it did, and we would have averted the severe emotional damage we did to each other. However, the upside of being with him became the conduit through which I came to *know* myself. I thank God every day for the life experience I gained during the time I spent with Ed.

Early in our courtship, I remember one date, in particular, that should have registered with me as a reason to not get serious about him. It was when we were at McDonald's, and he told me to order what I wanted. As I was telling the clerk I wanted French fries, Ed interrupted me to say he wasn't paying for the fries because they weren't healthy for me, adding that eating them was like drinking a vat of grease. I was shocked by his comment and his refusal to pay for the fries but didn't make a scene. I nicely reminded him that I was a grown-up and could eat whatever I wanted to eat whether he approved or not. Ed agreed but still said he wasn't paying for my fries. That incident was very telling, but I didn't pay close enough attention to the behavior he displayed as I should have.

Another telling incident of Ed's insensitivity to me that I, once again, overlooked was following my gallbladder surgery. When I was released from the hospital and went home, I asked Ed—as he was on his way over to see me—if he would pick up breakfast for me from my favorite spot, the Waffle House. I asked him to get me some grits, bacon, toast with butter, and scrambled eggs with cheese. He refused outright to pick up the breakfast I asked for because, as he put it, *I didn't need to eat all that grease*. I was so angry with him for not being more sensitive to me especially since I had just gotten out of the hospital. My craving for that breakfast was so strong that I got out of my sickbed, drove myself to the Waffle House, and bought my own breakfast.

Admittedly, Ed was correct in what he said about the grease (especially since I no longer had a gall bladder), but his adamant insensitivity to me by not even suggesting an alternative breakfast he could bring me was very hurtful. Ed was a former health director and very knowledgeable about food and the body. However, his approach in telling me about the foods I liked that were bad for me was so hard-core that his well-meaning message was drowned out and came across as controlling. We had ourselves a spirited argument after that. I felt he could have indulged me that one time since I was sick; especially since I usually catered to his every wish when he was at my home most weekends.

About eight months into our relationship, Ed brought up the suggestion that we live together. I immediately replied that would not happen unless we were married. At that point, I should have asked God for his direction on this relationship and seriously seek his will for my life. But I didn't pray about my situation with Ed, but leaned on my own understanding. Consequently, I couldn't blame anyone but myself for the troubles I faced in that relationship. Sadly, Ed never proposed to me. I was the one who steered our relationship to the altar. I picked out a ring I liked and Ed bought it for me.

When Ed and I met, I lived in Durham and worked at the Duke Medical Center, which was 20 minutes from my job. Ed lived thirty-five miles away in Alamance county. He suggested we look for a house to rent closer to his family. I agreed. We found a lovely little home and rented it. My ride to Duke became a thirty-five mile commute. We moved in together three weeks before our wedding. My family was not happy about my decision to marry Ed, and thought it strange that he had never come to Baltimore with me to meet them during our courtship. In his defense, I would always reply that he was a nice guy, and they just needed to get to know him.

The Saturday I moved from Durham to our marriage home, it was raining cats and dogs. Ed did not help me with the move from my fully furnished townhouse in Durham to that rental home in Graham—some thirty-five miles away—but went to work that day and left me on my own to fend for myself. Ed had been living with his mother when I met him, and only had a king size bed and his clothes to move into the house. I felt abandoned and insignificant when Ed did not help me with the move. Although I felt trapped and unloved, it never occurred to me to pull out of that relationship because I wanted to make it work.

I ignored and overlooked the fact that Ed never discussed helping with any of the expenses for our marriage ceremony. He even collected half of the fee from me when we went to get our marriage license. I should have come to my senses that this was not a good situation for me, but I didn't. I'm not exactly sure why I resorted to secretly applying for a credit card in Ed's name to pay for the wedding, but it seemed like a good idea at the time since I planned to pay off the bill before Ed found out what I had done. Clearly I was either mentally deranged, a pitiful and lonely soul, or I wanted to be married so badly that I compromised good values for bad choices. I bought my dress, ordered invitations, bought Ed's ring, and pulled together a modest ceremony for about $1,500, which I charged on that credit card. The marriage ceremony was set for the Thanksgiving weekend of 1993. All my family came to North Carolina for the ceremony, and two of my lifelong girlfriends also made the trip. The day of the wedding, torrential rain fell all day long.

After we were married, more red flags appeared but I had to lie in the hard bed I had just made for myself. On our wedding day, we received over $700 in cash gifts. Ed asked me to give him half of the money to pay *his* property taxes for some land that he owned. Over the weeks and months that followed, it became crystal clear to me that I had made a serious mistake to marry Ed. I tried hard to ignore my unhappiness and climbed deeper and deeper into depression. My husband, the food police, continued nagging me about eating the foods he disapproved of so I began hiding from him when I ate fried drumsticks, sweet potato pie, or potato chips. Oddly, if I happened to eat anything in front of Ed that he disapproved of, he actually accused me of deliberately provoking him. Then we'd end up arguing. Now mind you, I was not an obese or plump woman, so I could not understand my husband's obsession with what I ate. Actually, I was still a *fox* who could turn a few heads even though I really didn't feel attractive.

I never believed that Ed loved me, so I constantly tried to do everything I knew how to make him like me. I kept a neat home for him, cooked him good meals, and generally never refused him. All we basically had was a vibrant sex life, but that was not enough to make me feel okay about myself or the relationship. I finally went to Ed and asked him if we could go to marriage counseling because I had some serious issues going on. His response was disappointing. He refused and said he wasn't willing to share his personal business with a stranger. At that point, I had to suck up my pride and push past my pain. Maybe if I were a drinking woman, I could have drowned my pain in booze; instead, I shopped and shopped and shopped to stop hurting inside. Over time, I racked up $30,000 of credit card debt on Ed's cards without his knowledge. I bought stuff for our house, lavish Christmas gifts for his family, and lots of stuff for him. Perhaps Ed thought I had money and that he had struck pay dirt marrying me since he never questioned where I was getting the money to buy the things he saw me come home with.

One day, my secret unraveled when a creditor called Ed at work about a missed payment on that credit card I acquired to pay for our wedding. Needless to say, he was livid when he came home from work and confronted me. Here was an *Oh! Jesus* moment second to none! I confessed that I had used all his credit cards, as well as mine, to buy stuff. Then the profane floodgates of verbal abuse out of Ed's mouth opened with a vengeance. Whenever he thought about what I had done, he would get angry all over again and berate me with such foul language until I felt totally worthless. I admitted to him that I was depressed and needed professional help, but my pleas to Ed fell on deaf ears. He actually told me I could think myself happy.

Ed wanted us to own a home but told me I had hijacked his financial future, and owning a home was no longer possible given the amount of debt I had put us in. I made the payments on all the credit card debt I had made solely from my income and bore the total financial burden and took responsibility for the mess I made. I was hurting so badly inside and there was no where I found refuge. What I wanted to hear my husband say to me more than anything else was something comforting like "Although I am not happy about what you did, we are a team in this together, and we will get through it together." Instead, the cursing continued.

Because of what I had done, I realized I could not stay in my marriage with the constant climate of anger and profane abuse I was receiving. During one of Ed's calmer moments, I assured him that I would help him get a house whether he believed it could happen or not. The first thing I did was pray and ask God to help me fix the mess I had made and to show me what to do. Next I began researching ways to make that happen. I wanted to redeem myself so my husband wouldn't remember me as a bad person. But most of all, I wanted to help him buy a home because I knew I would be leaving him. A week after I cried to God, I had a dream about houses. When the Realtor showed us the house we ultimately bought, I knew it was the right one the minute I walked inside because I saw signs in my dream to let me know what to look for. As confirmation that we selected the right house, the street signs at the corner of the block cross-spelled both of my Dad's names. The realtor gave us the application; I took everything home and got started on the paperwork.

Once again, I pulled out my trusty typewriter and completed all the paperwork. My aim was to assemble the financial packet in such an organized manner that would really impress the lender. Ed's credit was stellar because I maintained a good payment record despite the volume of debt I had loaded him up with. We were approved for the mortgage in just two weeks, which is unheard of. The mortgage company later told us they were so impressed with the way I put together our application that it was a breeze processing our loan. God's grace was at work for me again. We moved into the house thirty days later.

Things between my husband and me were okay for a while because he finally had another home of his own. I took on two additional part-time jobs to make sure I could keep up the payments on those bills I had made. Ed paid the mortgage and a few other household bills. Our arguments over money continued despite all my attempts to keep our household running smoothly. Ultimately, I sought assistance from a credit counseling service that negotiated reduced interest rates and monthly payments on all of our collective debt. Their intervention was a saving grace for me. I made one monthly payment to them, and they paid all the creditors under an agreed schedule. The time projection they gave us for being completely debt free was five years. I knew I could not handle five more years of verbal abuse from my husband. I could not see how or when I would leave Ed, but I knew I had to leave the marriage if I wanted to hang onto my sanity.

Several things happened next that finally shook me to my senses. In addition to continually being cursed and verbally abused over the debt issue, I had been so blind to the blatant selfishness I put up with while we were together. However, after a major family blowup during Christmas of 1997, I told Ed to his face that I was leaving him. I wasn't sure how or when, but he could bank on it. I knew we were on borrowed time and asked God to help me get to a peaceful place in my life. I repented for being disobedient, vowed to live a better life, and waited on the door that only he could open for me. Four months later, my daughter had to have a major surgery; so I agreed to go to Maryland, stay with her for ten days, and help out during her recovery. As the time drew closer, I began to ask myself, *Why should I even come back?* Once that light bulb went off in my head, I was crystal clear on my plan. I called my son, who was in his last year of university, to tell him I was going to Maryland to take care of Pam, I was also leaving Ed and not coming back to Carolina. That meant I would no longer be the close insulation to my baby boy that he was used to having. Once again, Phillip encouraged me to do what I had to do because he completely understood what I had been going through since the Christmas blowup also involved him. Phillip assured me he would be okay and promised he would finish school that year.

The week before I left to go to my daughter's, I started gathering everything my car could hold in one trip and hid all of it in a closet that Ed never looked in. I also resigned from my three jobs. I assembled my files and packed them neatly in a container so I could take everything with me and continue paying the bills on time. When the day came for me to leave, I waited for my husband to go to work, and I started packing my car. It took me three hours to position my stuff in the trunk and inside the car. I could only see out of my side view mirrors because I packed my car right up to the ceiling, which blocked my ability to see out of the back window. I straightened up the house, ate some lunch, said a prayer, and locked the door as I left. I had $20 in my pocket and a full tank of gas to get me to Baltimore. I drove out of my driveway and never looked back.

I arrived at my daughter's house six hours later, thanking God for watching over me. Next I unloaded my car and breathed a huge sigh of relief that all was well. I cooked, cleaned, and helped Pam stay comfortable while she recuperated. I had been away from my family for ten years, and I knew that I would have to rebuild some of those relationships again, especially the one with my daughter. Although she was a grown woman and on her own when I moved to North Carolina, having me close by when she needed her mom was not a comfort that she enjoyed while I was away. However, my sister stepped up to the plate and filled some of that void as her aunt.

Four days after arriving at my daughter's house, Ed called and asked me when was I coming home. I told him to have a seat because there was something I needed to tell him. He said, "What?"

And I said, "In answer to your question, I'm *not* coming back home because I've left you. I will return at a later date to pack up the rest of my things, and I will be happy to sign the house over to you." There was a long pause on the other end of the phone; then he said okay and hung up.

I knew I had to find a job, so I prayed and asked God to help me with that. The next week, I located a temp agency in the Yellow Pages and registered with them. The very nice counselor that helped me with my job search became a dear friend with whom I have kept in contact with over the years. Jane sent me on an interview with a prestigious law firm and something happened that hasn't happened to me since I was sixteen; I was hired *on the spot* and asked to report for work that Monday. And here's the best part—the salary I was given was enough that I didn't have to work part-time anymore. I was beside myself with joy because it had been three years since I was able to be home after my 5:00 PM shift ended—I was so used to going to another job and working an additional four or five hours. That *Oh! Jesus* moment was awesome!

Once Ed was convinced I really wasn't coming back to him, he retained a lawyer and began divorce proceedings. Since I willingly gave Ed my interest in our house, his lawyer prepared the papers for me to sign. I drove back to Carolina two months after leaving my husband and signed the deed transfer papers at his lawyer's office. Next he met me at the house while I packed and removed some of my remaining things that I then put into storage until I had my own place. My plan was for my sister and me to drive to Carolina in my car, rent a large truck, and drive the truck back to Maryland with all my furniture that I left in the house and those things I had put in storage. After working at the law firm for three months, I had saved up enough money to get my own apartment and execute my plan.

A wonderful lady I met and developed a friendship with during one of the temporary assignments I worked in Carolina was the person God used as the glue to hold my plan together. Three months later my sister and I went to Carolina to permanently move all my stuff back to Baltimore. Sadie asked two of her male friends to help me. Sadie's two helpers met me at Ed's house that August and packed my rental truck just like two professional movers. Next they unloaded my storage unit and added its contents to the truck. I was on pure adrenaline as I drove the truck back to Baltimore. Dee followed behind the truck driving my car. We arrived in Baltimore late the night of August 14, 1998. I immediately got down on my knees and kissed the floor of my new home. I thanked God for safely bringing me to a new life. After I ended my marriage in 1998, I embraced a life of solitude so I could begin to heal. Four months after I moved back to Maryland, my son graduated from university with his highest grade point average ever. My *baby* moved to California and began his life as a successful software executive.

Although my third (and final) marriage did not work and was a serious lesson in futility, I am eternally grateful for the experiences I had with Ed. It was during my relationship with him that I came to clearly understand myself better and the reasons behind the *dark* things I have done throughout my life. First, I learned that my discontent with men and my view of them—as insignificant creatures—were directly connected to my Dad. Apparently I had never really gotten past the pain of him not rescuing me from my mother when I got pregnant as a teenager. Somehow, I had buried a deep contempt for him—even though I didn't know that I had—and that contempt transferred itself to every man I got close to and ultimately emasculated.

The dishonest things I did were because I learned that characteristic from my mother. There is a Chinese proverb that says, "A child's life is like a piece of paper on which every person leaves a mark." My mother left an indelible mark on me that I suppressed from my memory for almost all my life.

> *(When I was about eight years old, my mother saw $400 in my Dad's dresser drawer. I saw her take it, and she told me not to tell. When my Dad discovered his money was gone and asked Mom about it, she told him that two friends of mine were in his room with me playing, and perhaps one of them took his money. That night, my Dad gave me the worst beating I've ever had for something I didn't do. He beat me for having company in his room, and that was not what happened. My mother stole his money and lied on me.)*

Also because of my mother, I have not allowed myself to develop close friendships with women because of a suppressed distrust for females that has been inside me all those years. The relationship I have with my sister is the only one that ever mattered to me and the only one I valued. She has always accepted me as I am, mixed up as I may have been, but I know she is my safe harbor.

When I left my husband in April of 1998, I knew what it felt like to hate a human being. But God healed me of that horrible sin and filled my heart with nothing but love for Ed. Over the years since our marriage ended, we have become good friends. We talk regularly by phone. Because Ed has such a quest for knowledge, we enjoy spirited discussions about many things. We've admitted to each other how ironic it is how we now communicate with each other better than we did when we were married. If I ever have an intellectual dilemma, Ed is the person I call for the right answer. I completely understand him now. While I don't know if Ed has ever forgiven me for the money and credit problem I caused him, I do know that I did my best by him—such as it was—given the emotional baggage I carried into our marriage. Nonetheless, I wish him all the best that life has to offer.

Ed still lives in the house we bought together, and over time, he has come to appreciate how easy I made it look to take care of our home and not nag him to help out with any of the chores. A year after our divorce, I turned the bills back over to Ed to finish paying; I figured it was an equitable exchange since he had the house.

I am very glad there were situations and events I went through during my life that clearly became channels for me to regurgitate the pain I had buried in the dark recesses of my soul. Now after writing this book, I understand why (1) I warred against men, (2) I distanced myself from females, and (3) I did dishonest things. Telling my story has allowed me to remove the Band-Aids that have covered my scars. God has healed my mind and restored my child-like spirit. I have made tremendous strides in becoming a better person and I must give God all the glory for helping me over all the humps of my rainbow.

While I'm sure I did not meet all Ed's needs, seriously disappointed him and perhaps destroyed his trust in women, I nonetheless wish him nothing but happiness and pray that one day God will heal his heart of the anguish I caused him.

I am so blessed to have raised three very successful children, who each blessed me with two grandchildren for a total of six. My daughter, Pamela, has a stellar career as a manager with the government, and is gifted with the coveted talent of bringing out the best in her people. She is married to an outstanding man who makes me so proud. They have a son and a daughter, and he is a wonderful Dad to them. Moreover, he loves my baby girl as God commands a man to love his wife. Despite my poor example with relationships, I remind my daughter regularly how proud I am of her for staying the course and overcoming snags when her marriage hits a bump in the road. (She surely didn't learn that from me.)

My baby boy, Phillip, is a very successful business development manager. His job enables him to travel the world as he brings home the bacon to the angel he is married to that God sent him when he lived in California. She embodies the true spirit of Godly compassions and is the perfect wife who is an outstanding mother and homemaker. They have two beautiful children—a daughter and a son—who bring them so much joy.

My oldest son, Paisley, went on to get an MBA from the Wharton school of business and worked on Wall Street for five years. He too is very successful and has two beautiful children—also a son and daughter. Within the next year, I will gain another beautiful daughter-in-law when he and his fiancé are married.

God has never failed me despite all the roads I've traveled and all the messes I've made throughout my life. I look at my children—my legacy—and clearly see that God's hand has been on my life because the evidence of His goodness is all around me. Had it not been for my relationship with God, I'd *still* be stuck on the hump of my rainbow.

Life is wonderful for me now; and when I go to live with Christ, I want my epitaph to read, "**Whoa, Nellie, what a ride!**"

* * *

I have learned that . . .

- **How you start is not where you end** *(see Philippians 3:13-14)*

    ^{13} . . . but this one thing I do, forgetting those things which are behind, and reaching forth unto those things which are before, ^{14}I press toward the mark for the prize of the high calling of God in Christ Jesus.

- **The Word of God is life's *real* instruction book** *(see Psalm 119:105)*

    Thy word is a lamp unto my feet, and a light unto my path.

- **The peace that comes from knowing God *does* exceed human comprehension** *(see Philippians 4:7)*

    And the peace of God, which passeth all understanding, shall keep your hearts and minds through Christ Jesus.

Epilogue

I have paid very high prices—which I call consequences—for some of the bad choices I have made throughout my life. Although not all my decisions were prudent ones, lessons were learned from each. The experiences that I have shared in this book will help you know that nothing in life is insurmountable. More importantly, learning how to forgive is *Key* to living a wholesome life; you only do harm to yourself if you hold onto unforgiveness. Scripture is clear on forgiveness as stated in Matthew chapter 6, verse 12 (*And forgive us our debts, as we also have forgiven [left, remitted, and let go of the debts, and have given up resentment against] our debtors*).

Although frustration is the spark that starts the fire of anger, *do not* stay angry with anyone or over anything. I had to forgive several people for heart-wrenching situations that severely impacted my life. I resisted forgiving those folk for a long time and it took a serious toll on me. Finally, with God's help, I can truly say that my heart is full of Godly love for every person that hurt me throughout my life. I am a better person for letting go of the anger that took root in my soul.

If I can learn forgiveness, so can you. The rewards have been endless as God continues to bless me every single day that I journey along the *roads* of my rainbow.

* * *

Index

A

AA treatment program, 156
abortion, 54, 65, 74, 114, 155
Acapulco, 147
Adonis, 101
African American women,
    sterilization of, 138
allotment disbursements, 69
American Express Card, 152
Art (insurance agent), 110, 111, 112,
    113, 114, 122, 123, 127, 128
Atlas Van Lines, 166

B

Bahamas, 123
Baisden, Michael, 138
Baltimore, Maryland, 13, 21, 62, 65,
    118, 164, 165, 167, 171, 174, 176
Band-Aid, 137, 144, 177
bankruptcy, 151
Beethoven, Ludwig van
    Moonlight Sonata, 34
Bennett (sergeant), 65

Bible, 27, 28, 34, 82
    miracles of, 30
    stories of, 30
Big Paisley. *See* Dad (father)
birthdays, 49, 63, 64, 96, 97, 120,
    133, 137, 147, 170
Blue Cross Blue Shield,
Brown. *See* Brown University
Brown (piano player), 38, 39, 62
Brown University, 162, 163, 164, 167

C

California, 176, 178
car accident, 92
career day, 46
Carmen Jones (film), 112
Carolina. *See* North Carolina
castor oil, 121
Chan, Charlie, 117
Chapel Hill, North Carolina, 165, 166
Charlie (boyfriend), 132, 133, 134, 135
Chevy
    Chevette, 153
    Impala, 64
    Malibu, 71

child support, 128, 129
choir, 37, 39
Christmas, 19, 26, 47, 62, 64, 91, 94, 135, 140, 141, 142, 143, 152, 164, 172, 174
cloaking, 107
College Hill (Providence, Rhode Island), 163
Commander. *See* Hulbert, Maurice
Connors, Chuck, 147
Contemporary (hotel in Walt Disney World), 130
Country Bear Jamboree, 130
Cromer (doctor), 137

D

Dad (father), 13, 14, 15, 17, 18, 21, 24, 25, 31, 32, 33, 34, 39, 51, 53, 54, 56, 65, 68, 85, 92, 94, 106, 107, 115, 120, 121, 122, 136, 137, 138, 139, 140, 142, 143, 148, 150
David, 30
DC. *See* Washington DC
Dear John letter, 75
Dee (sister), 14, 15, 16, 17, 18, 19, 20, 21, 22, 24, 25, 30, 33, 37, 44, 46, 49, 50, 51, 56, 59, 61, 75, 95, 97, 113, 121, 122, 123, 140, 145, 146, 155, 165, 176
Department of Defense, 62
Detroit, Michigan, 146, 148
Diamond Jim, 115, 116
disappointment, 128
Disney World, 129, 130
divine thread, 79
divorce, 74, 76, 93, 146, 147, 148, 152, 169
Doctors Hospital, 137
Donald Duck, 130
Duke Botanical Gardens, 169
Durham, North Carolina, 171
DWI (driving while intoxicated), 156

E

East Side (Providence, Rhode Island), 163
Easter break, 52
Eastern Air Lines, 130
Ed (third husband), 169, 170, 171, 172, 174, 175, 176
Edmondson Village, 25
education
    elementary, 31
    high school, 45, 46
    junior high school, 37
    kindergarten, 20, 21
80/20 rule, 149
embezzlement, 115, 116
Equitable Trust Bank, 130
exodus, 63, 65, 93

F

Fathers Day, 121, 143
Florida, 129
food stamps, 138
forgiveness, 77
Fortune 500, 160
Francis (music teacher), 34, 35
free will, 9, 10
Friendship Baptist, 38, 39

G

Gist (deacon), 38
God, 9, 10, 26, 27, 28, 32, 39, 40, 51, 56, 70, 75, 77, 79, 82, 91, 94, 95, 96, 98, 99, 101, 102, 104, 114, 116, 123, 125, 128, 129, 130, 136, 139, 141, 151, 154, 155, 156, 157, 158, 160, 161, 162, 163, 167, 171, 173, 174, 175, 176, 177, 178
Gossett, Louis, Jr., 119
grace, 125
Graham, Billy, 158
Greyhound bus station, 82

H

hacking, 107
heaven, 26, 27
Henri (father of aborted baby), 46, 48, 49, 50, 51, 52, 53, 54, 57, 58, 61, 68
Hill (supervisor), 164, 165, 166
Hillsborough, North Carolina, 164, 165
hopscotch, 31, 32, 33, 34
Hot Rod. *See* Hulbert, Maurice;*See* Hulbert, Maurice
Hulbert, Maurice, 117, 118, 119, 120, 121, 122, 123, 128, 130
hurdles, 162
hysterectomy, 138

I

infidelity, 74, 76, 82
Ivy League colleges, 162

J

Jane (counselor), 175
Jesus Christ, 19, 25, 26, 27, 29, 30, 32, 35, 38, 39, 52, 55, 62, 79, 156, 158, 161, 178
jobs
    church organist, 38, 39, 44, 65
    clerk typist, 89
    executive secretary, 100, 130
    housekeeper, 44, 45
    junior typist, 60
    Saturday job, 33
Juanita (aunt), 15

K

Kelvinator, 44
Ku Klux Klan, 165
K Street, 133

L

Labor Day, 139
Lila (friend from church), 63
Little Feel. *See* Phillip (younger son)
Little Pais. *See* Paisley (older son)
Little Paisley. *See* Paisley (older son)
Little Phillip. *See* Phillip (younger son)
Looking Out for Number One (Ringer), 149
lung cancer, 120, 136

M

Maggie (Moms midwife), 14, 15, 16
Marco (rapist), 44, 45, 50, 51, 103
Maryland, 31, 32, 33, 61, 65, 162, 165, 174, 175
Maryland State Hopscotch Championship, 32
McDonalds, 161, 162, 170
"me, myself, and I" mode, 149
Meade, Fort, 89
medical insurance, 70, 75
Me-me (Dees daughter), 146
Michael (junior high crush), 37
Mickey Mouse, 130
Minnie (aunt), 15
mixing board, 46, 48, 49, 50, 101
Mom (mother), 13, 14, 15, 17, 19, 20, 21, 22, 23, 24, 25, 28, 29, 32, 33, 34, 36, 37, 38, 39, 50, 51, 52, 53, 54, 55, 56, 57, 58, 60, 93, 107, 122, 139, 154, 155, 156, 176
Montezumas revenge, 147
Moonlight Sonata (Beethoven), 34, 35
mortgage, approval of, 173
Mother Nature, 121

N

"Nearer, My God, to Thee", 34
Negro, 60
Nezzie (cousin), 36
911, 155
North Carolina, 16, 61, 62, 75, 164, 165, 166, 167, 168, 171, 175, 176, 177
Nova, 113

O

O'Jays, 101
Oh! Jesus moments, 9, 10, 21, 22, 23, 30, 32, 38, 51, 76, 82, 116, 141, 158, 172
Old Testament, 30
Open Heart Singers, 62
Orlando, Florida, 129, 130
OW (friend met while grocery shopping), 95, 97, 98, 99

P

Pais. See Paisley (older son)
Paisley (author's father's name), 15, 16
Paisley (older son), 92, 93, 113, 114, 120, 121, 122, 123, 129, 130, 136, 144, 148, 152, 154, 158, 160, 161, 162, 163, 164, 166, 167
Pam. See Pamela (daughter)
Pamela (daughter), 86, 88, 89, 91, 93, 113, 120, 121, 123, 129, 130, 144, 148, 154, 158, 159, 160, 175
paternity petition, 128
Pennsylvania, 163
Pentecostal church, 84
Phil. See Phillip (younger son)
Philadelphia, Pennsylvania, 37, 118
Phillip (younger son), 122, 123, 127, 128, 129, 131, 135, 144, 145, 146, 147, 152, 154, 158, 160, 162, 164, 165, 166, 174
piano
    lessons, 34
    playing of, 35, 37, 38
    progress on, 34
    recital, 34, 35, 39
Pisces, 133, 146
plan of salvation, 26
Polynesian Village
    (hotel in Walt Disney World), 130

pregnancy, 15, 51, 52, 53, 54, 64, 68, 75, 76, 86, 91, 114, 116, 117, 119, 121, 127
prom, 61, 62
promiscuity, 79, 109
Providence, Rhode Island, 163, 164
Providence River, 163
Prudential Insurance, 110
PSAT (Preliminary SAT), 160

R

radiation, 120, 136
radio broadcasting, 44
radium cobalt treatments, 120
Radmann (doctor), 121, 122
rainbow, definition of, 9
Randallstown, Maryland, 115, 154
rape, 45, 46, 48, 51, 103, 104, 105, 106
Ratliffs (family employer), 45
Ratliff (former employer), 44
Rawls, Lou, 119
Reads drugstore, 152
Rhode Island, 164
Rifleman (of *The Rifleman*), 147
Rimp (boyfriend), 151, 152, 153, 154, 156, 157, 158
Ringer, Robert
    Looking Out for Number One, 149
RJ (rapist), 101, 102, 103, 104, 105, 106, 107, 108, 109, 110, 111, 112, 113
Roberts, Oral, 25
    revival, 24, 25, 28, 29, 158
Rod. See Hulbert, Maurice
Rods Girl Friday, 119
"Roddism", 119
Ronii (authors nickname), 164
Ronnie (name of aborted baby), 56
Russell (dirtiest boy in class), 20, 21

S

Sack (first husband), 62, 64, 65, 69, 70, 74, 75, 76, 81, 82, 83, 84, 85, 86, 87, 88, 91, 92, 93, 94, 96, 97, 98, 99, 114, 122, 130, 143, 147
Sadie (friend), 176
Sampson. *See* Henri
SAT, 160
Satan, 79
science project, 31, 32
senior choir anniversary, 62
Sharon (friend), 167, 168
Sheena, Queen of the Jungle, 109
Shoff (ex-fiancé), 61, 62, 63, 64, 70, 71, 72, 73, 74, 75, 82
shorthand, 45, 46
Sinai Hospital, 121
Sleeper, 169
Solomon, 30
Spencer (boarder), 22
Spinners, 101
sterilization, 138, 139
Straw (supervisor), 89, 90
Sturdivant (fifth-grade science teacher), 31, 32
Sunday school, 18, 19, 30, 38
Sybil (name author calls Tish), 140

T

"teddy bear" arrangement, 102
Texas, 149
Thanksgiving, 62, 108, 140, 161, 171
Tish (supervisor), 140
Tom (second husband), 144, 145, 146, 147, 148, 149, 150, 152, 164
track, 161, 162
tubal ligation, 137
TV sports, 135
20/20 vision, 150
typing, 37, 43, 45, 46, 61, 132

U

Uncle Sam, 63, 69
University of Maryland, 119
University of North Carolina, 166
UPS, 149

V

Valentines Day, 51
vandalism, 97
Vee (author's name), 16, 28, 30, 39, 52, 60, 104, 107, 110, 115, 121, 137, 138, 151
Velveeta cheese, 33
Vietnam, 65, 67, 68, 75, 82
    Vietnam War, 64
Villanova University, 163
Virginia, 65
VOSA (voice of sound advice), 117, 119
Vuanita (author's middle name), 16, 140

W

Waffle House, 170
Wall Street, 178
Wallace (counselor), 32
Walt Disney, 130
want ads, 60, 100, 167
    Washington DC, 54, 113, 130, 132, 137, 139
Websters Dictionary, 9
wedding, 30, 58, 63, 64, 65, 68, 69, 70, 71, 76, 81, 82, 85, 147, 148, 171
West Coast, 133
Wharton school of business, 178
Whitmans chocolates, 122
WITH (radio station in Baltimore), 118